UNDERSTANDING CHILDREN

SECOND EDITION

Jeannette Harrison

arena

First published 1991 by The Australian Council for Educational Research Ltd, 19 Prospect Hill Road, Camberwell, Melbourne, Victoria 3124, Australia. Reprinted 1991, 1993, 1994. Second edition 1996.

This edition published by
Arena
Ashgate Publishing Limited
Gower House
Croft Road
Aldershot
Hants GU11 3HR
England

Ashgate Publishing Company
Old Post Road
Brookfield
Vermont 05036
USA

British Library Cataloguing in Publication Data

Harrison, Jeanette
    Understanding children – 2nd edn
    1. Child psychology 2. Children and adults
    I.Title
    155.4

Library of Congress Catalog Card Number: 96-85965

ISBN 1 85742 387 9

Cover design by Caro Designworks
Designed by Noni Edmunds
Photography by Bill Thomas
Typeset by Butler Graphics Pty Ltd
Printed by Biddles Ltd, Guildford

▦ C O N T E N T S ▦

F O R E W O R D

The need for a book which applies the theory of Adlerian psychology to infants and very young children has been apparent for
many years. Most of the existing materials available to caregivers
have dealt with older children and with adolescents.

Further, the shortage of materials which are directed towards
the needs of child-care and day-care workers has been obvious,
particularly as this area has grown rapidly in the past few years.

Jeannette Harrison has written a book which will be welcomed
by parents and professionals who have the responsibility of caring
for very young children. Focusing on the importance of positive
relationships and based on the psychology of Alfred Adler, the
book gives parents and caregivers a sound theoretical framework
for understanding and influencing children, a wide variety of
practical examples, and ample activities for further learning and
skill building.

The book also incorporates some developmental approaches
which indicate appropriate age-related activities for children,
introduces the reader to communication strategies, and offers a
comprehensive strategy for 'making it work' for the caregiver.

I welcome the addition of this book to the expanding range of resources which are designed to help parents and caregivers with the nurturing of children, and particularly welcome this book which focuses on infants and very young children. Its positive and encouraging message will be warmly appreciated by all readers.

PROFESSOR MAURICE BALSON,
DIRECTOR,
MONASH PARENT–TEACHER EDUCATION CENTRE

September, 1990

PREFACE TO SECOND EDITION

The first edition of *Understanding Children: Towards Responsive Relationships* has been widely used by parents, teachers and carers of children of all ages. Many readers have provided valuable feedback and encouragement, even describing the positive impact it has made on their own interactions with children. This was my original intent in writing the book, and this purpose also remains unchanged for the second edition. I wish to promote responsive relationships and enhanced communication between adults and children. This can only be achieved through providing relevant knowledge about appropriate adult attitudes and effective guidance strategies.

There has been much world-wide emphasis on contemporary caregiving and parenting practices recently. In writing a second edition, I have been responsive to an increased demand for information on self-esteem, positive communication and conflict resolution. New chapters are included on each of these areas. Further, there are additional chapters on the use of encouraging language, and cross-cultural implications arising from different child-care techniques.

Understanding Children: Towards Responsive Relationships (second edition) retains its sequential approach to learning new information, effectively enabling the reader to continue building on existing skills and knowledge.

This second edition is dedicated to the readers of my book and participants of my training programs, for their valuable ideas and encouragement in supporting a new approach to understanding children. I thank them for their inspiration to continue writing and teaching. As in the first edition, I again offer readers my encouragement for warm and nurturing relationships with children. The children are our future!

JEANNETTE HARRISON

PREFACE TO FIRST EDITION

The idea of writing *Understanding Children* developed from my personal involvement and commitment to understanding and guiding the behaviour of babies and young children, and from the support and encouragement of my colleagues in the Department of Child Care Studies at Prahran College of TAFE.

As a parent, teacher and caregiver, I have become increasingly aware of the dilemma facing those working with children. How can we best provide an appropriate environment to allow children freedom to be themselves and be understood, to develop responsible and independent attitudes whilst maintaing limits and supervisory control?

Understanding Children is designed to develop skills of understanding and guidance of children's behaviour for those interacting with young children. It is possible for it to be used as a supplement to training courses for students, as a resource book and learning program for staff in child-care centres and kindergartens or by individual parents and other adults wishing to develop understanding and skills in effective guidance of young children. The term 'caregiver' refers to any person having significant interaction with children, in either a paid or unpaid capacity, including parents, grandparents or early childhood workers.

The focus in *Understanding Children* is on developing in the reader or group participant an understanding of Individual Psychology, so that they can better understand and guide the behaviour of children and babies. However, no matter what skills and knowledge are acquired, none of these will be effective unless sensitive and responsive interactions are established early in a relationship. Hence, the reader will find emphasis on a democratic relationships approach with children, parents and other caregivers.

The infants and young children described in this book are girls, except in some examples. This has been done intentionally because in the past 'he' has dominated most books about young children. By using 'she' and not the traditional 'he', I wish to redress this imbalance and encourage the reader to regard each child as a unique individual and worthwhile human being.

A set of Guidelines is included at the conclusion of the book for those who wish to use *Understanding Children* as a structured learning program for either in-service programs or teaching purposes.

This book is all for those adults who have the courage to work towards more responsive relationships with the young children in their lives. I offer you, the reader, my encouragement towards the satisfaction of responsive and effective caregiving of young children.

JEANNETTE HARRISON

■ S E C T I O N   I ■

UNDERSTANDING CHILDREN: A NEW APPROACH

Focus

A constructive framework through which to understand young children will offer caregivers a feeling of security from an informed knowledge base. Society's attitudes to children are changing, as are the children and families themselves. The need to sensitively and effectively respond to these challenges with alternative ideas has never been more obvious than today.

1

*T*HE SECRET OF SELF-ESTEEM

I believe the children are the future . . .
Teach them well
And let them lead the way
Show them all the beauty they possess inside
Give them a sense of pride
(Whitney Houston, 'The Greatest Love of All'
© Linda Creed, 1977)

Self-esteem

Our children are the future, and that future is dependent on how children are treated, respected and valued — now. The manner in which adults interact with children today will affect these children and others, in their tomorrows.

We are learning more and more about the ongoing influence of self-esteem on children's development, beginning from early infancy onwards. In fact, research is demonstrating that their self-esteem will have a profound effect on their future. We know that children who think highly of themselves behave in ways that are responsible, constructive and positive. In contrast, children who do not feel worthwhile are more likely to behave in a destructive and irresponsible manner.

So, what is this thing we call self-esteem? Everyone is talking about it so much nowadays but do we really know what it is and what it does? We are not born with a particular self-concept, nor are we born with low or high self-esteem.

Self-esteem is an evaluation, a feeling — a basic sense of 'Who I am is okay'.

Every child is unique and will of course need to be considered slightly differently from another. We are born with certain individual personality characteristics, but it is what we and other people around us do with those characteristics that make us who and what we are. Thus a child's understanding of her 'self' will depend on interactions with others around her.

The awareness of who we are, that is, the awareness of self, is a learning process that takes place over a long period of time and is shaped by every event in our lives. Whether you are a parent or a caregiver, it is important for you to understand the influence you have on children. The responses that children receive for their behaviour will influence their self-esteem and will also influence whether or not they keep behaving in certain ways. These patterns of behaviour will be discussed later in this book.

As a responsive adult, the crucial thing is to be aware of self-esteem. It is important for young children to develop a positive sense of self in order to feel worthwhile. Children can then feel comfortable with themselves knowing they are okay as people. Responsive adults will accept a child as she is, although her un-acceptable behaviour may have to be redirected.

Positive feelings about ourselves have an incredible effect on our ability to realise our full potential in life. Have you ever thought that in all the world there is no one else exactly like you? You are unique. This is what makes you, you. We have to teach children that they are worthwhile, they are valuable, they are precious. We have to teach them to feel good about themselves: to develop self-acceptance. This is what self-esteem is about, and it is a part of our whole self-concept.

The notion of self-concept was originally studied in relation to the term 'looking glass self'. It described the way an individual's self-concept is determined not by the way the individual saw herself, but by the perceived reaction of others in the social situation. That is, how we think other people see us.

Self-concept describes the perceptions and the attitudes that a person has about themself. It refers to many aspects of self, including how we see our physical characteristics, our cognitive abilities, our gender, and also our identities. The development of the self-concept relies on information from our social environment through the interaction with others, particularly parents, teachers, siblings and peers. This will be described later in this book when you read about lifestyle perception.

Self-esteem, on the other hand is not just about how other people see us, but it refers to our personal judgement of our own worth — our self-acceptance. Self-esteem involves two components of self. The first is one's sense of worth and the other, a perception of one's competence. These factors are not necessarily equal in importance. In fact some researchers believe that a sense of inherent worth is the single most important factor in how we cope with life. It is affected by our interpretation of the way others see us.

The development of positive self-esteem involves a need for recognition from others. That is why a feeling of belonging is so important to children. Responsive adults need to respond to children in a warm and accepting manner by giving attention to children's acceptable behaviour and appropriate feedback for their negative behaviour. In order to feel worthwhile, children need adults who will demonstrate an accepting attitude rather than a judgemental view, and who will communicate in a clear and positive manner, thus giving children a strong sense of belonging.

The development of positive self-esteem is an ongoing process that has been shown to lead to children feeling more confident, accepting responsibility, adhering to rules and regulations more readily, and being respectful of others. The development of a positive sense of self can lead directly to the success of children later in their lives.

Self-esteem is therefore a major factor and a powerful influence on children's futures. We know that children who are cared for in a self-esteem enhancing environment are far more likely to be able to cope with problems later in life. They are usually confident and able to succeed knowing that they are okay even when they occasionally fail. Responsive adults who value self-esteem avoid judging children according to their success or failures.

A self-esteem enhancing approach will nurture children who feel good about themselves, and these children are less likely to behave in antisocial ways. There is a direct correlation between positive self-esteem and appropriate behaviour in children. Research studies show that children who have high self-esteem, that is, children who feel good about themselves, who feel accepted as they are and worthwhile, misbehave less. They develop self-discipline and responsibility. Whereas children with low self-esteem, that is, children who feel discouraged, or who feel less worthwhile than others, are more likely to misbehave and constantly show inappropriate behaviour.

Children can learn to be honest about their level of competence whilst being encouraged to feel comfortable about themselves. Self-esteem enables us to acknowledge strengths as well as vulnerabilities. Children with well established feelings of worth from infancy will develop a sense of personal acceptance together with confidence in their own abilities. These children will be those most likely to cope with life's future challenges.

Talking so simply about self-esteem may result in the development of unrealistic expectations. It is known that most adults and children fall somewhere in between the polarities of positive and negative. Self-esteem needs to be viewed as a lifelong process, the foundations of which are set down in early childhood by using a democratic approach with children, as described in Chapter 2.

There are skills adults can acquire and practise to enhance self-esteem development, but it is not always easy. As a parent, a caregiver or a teacher, it can often be difficult to consider our children and their feelings when we may not be feeling okay about ourselves. This can be one of the major challenges of adult-child interactions, and the strategies proposed in this book give guidelines for self-esteem enhancing interactions within a democratic approach. This is what responsive relationships are about. If we can acknowledge that effectively caring for children can be difficult and mistakes may be made, then we can move forward and ask

'How can I learn from what I just said or did?'. At times we need to reflect on our own behaviour, not just the children's.

Virginia Satir, in her book, *People Making*, stated, 'Feelings of worth can only flourish in an atmosphere where individual differences are appreciated, mistakes are tolerated, communication is open, rules are flexible — the kind of atmosphere that is found in a nurturing family'. This is the kind of democratic atmosphere that we want to create in any child care or family environment.

Responsive adults will be able to create a self-esteem enhancing approach where children feel accepted, confident and believed in.

How is self-esteem enhancing care provided?

Beginning in early infancy children need to have a feeling of their own inherent worth conveyed to them. An important factor in these early months is the sense of touch. Through touch, babies develop a symbiotic relationship with those around them, and begin to establish a sense of acceptance.

Research has shown that these early interactions have a profound effect on future behaviour. When babies are respectfully held, touched and nurtured, when their needs are met and adults respond positively to their cues, then these infants are likely to develop a strong sense of worth. They become trusting of their environments and establish positive behavioural patterns. These patterns form a template for their future lives. By providing an atmosphere where children feel accepted and worthwhile, the adult is enhancing the development of a more accepting and positive attitude towards others. A secure environment will increase children's confidence, competence and sense of worth.

We constantly communicate relationship messages which affect self-esteem. Adults need to be aware of how they are expressing their feelings and attitudes, what they are actually saying and the facial expression they are showing. Children will interpret these messages according to their perception of themselves, however adults can inadvertently reinforce negative perceptions.

Caregivers will foster the child's need to feel: 'I am special. There is no one else quite like me.'

A positive sense of worth

In order to develop a positive sense of worth children need to feel:

I am special. There is no one else quite like me.

When 2-year-old Guy walks into the playroom at his child care centre each day, Jackie, the caregiver, makes a point of stopping what she is doing in order to greet him. 'Good morning, Guy', she says, 'It's great to see you today.'

Responsive adults will ensure that each infant and child is greeted in a warm and friendly manner whenever they arrive in the room. Consider the strong sense of being valued that this gives a child: 'You actually stopped what you are doing to take notice of me. I didn't even have to misbehave to make you take notice'.

In some ways I am like other people, but I am also different, and that is okay.

At storytime a group of 3- and 4-year-olds are sitting with Scott, the caregiver, looking at a book about Aboriginal children. Scott is talking about the clothes the Aboriginal children are wearing and the food they are eating. Jeska, a 4-year-old says, 'Yuk. I don't like that.' Scott then initiates a discussion about different foods that these 3- and 4-year-olds like. They discover there are some things they all like and yet there are also lots of differences. 'Is that okay?' asks Scott, 'Is it all right to be the same in some things, but different in others?'

In all their interactions, children need to not only tolerate but to accept and respect differences. This will help children feel 'I do not have to be the same as everyone else to be accepted. I am unique and special.'

Some things are hard to do and some things I cannot do very well. But I am still okay.

It is important for the development of a positive sense of esteem that children are able to accept their level of competence and know that their worth is not judged on their abilities. Children so quickly develop a sense of failure and become discouraged by inappropriate messages such as, 'That puzzle is too hard for you Xenia. You need a simple one' or 'Xenia, you are so slow. Can't you even finish that puzzle?'

The responsive caregiver will instead give children a message that separates behaviour from the person, thus enabling a sense of worth. For example, Lucas is trying to construct his building so that it stays up like Carrie's, but it is not working and he is becoming frustrated and hits out at Carrie. Sophie, the caregiver quietly walks over and kneels beside Lucas, 'It is really annoying when you can't get things to work isn't it, Lucas? But I can't let you hurt Carrie. What could you do so that your building works the way you want?'

In this way, Sophie has respected Lucas's feeling of being unable, yet has still enabled him to feel accepted. Lucas will be given a feeling of, 'I can't do it as well as Carrie and I feel disappointed. Maybe my behaviour was not acceptable, but I know that Sophie still accepts me as a person.'

I am respected and through this I will learn how to demonstrate respect to other people.

When children feel worthwhile and valued themselves, they are far more likely to value and consider others. Children will model their behaviour on that of significant adults in their lives. Adults who can treat children as they themselves would like to be treated will find that children reciprocate this attitude.

Adults need to take children seriously and consider the feelings that are being expressed through certain behaviours. For example, Chia is sitting at the table, very involved with putting pieces of puzzle together. 'Tidy that up now, Chia' her Dad calls out, 'We are about to have dinner.' Chia looks up at him, showing him what she is doing. 'Put it away now, it's dinner time' says Dad. Chia quietly pushes the pieces of puzzle on to the floor and leaves the room.

Children need to know that their feelings are being considered, even if they cannot do what they want. Dad could have said to Chia, 'It looks like you're working hard at that puzzle. We'll need to clear the table for dinner soon, Chia, so what can you do about the puzzle?' or 'You're really enjoying doing that puzzle but we'll need to have dinner in a little while. I can see you'd love to keep going so you're welcome to do some more after dinner'.

In this way Chia can feel: 'I am being considered — my feelings are being valued. I still need to consider other people and work within limits, but I feel respected.'

My thoughts and ideas are important … I can listen to other people's ideas too, and respect them.

Children need to know we are listening to them in order to feel valued. Have you ever been having a conversation with another adult and you know, through their responses and body language that they are not listening. It makes you feel unimportant doesn't it? Well, it is the same for children. A shrug and an 'uh-huh' are not enough. Children will learn to listen respectfully to others when they are truly listened to themselves.

Instead of saying, 'uh-huh', 'really', or 'mmm', really think about what children are expressing, and respond to that. For example, when 4-year-old Jake was telling Tess, his caregiver, about going to the movies at the weekend it would have been very easy for Tess to appear to be listening by 'mm's' and 'really's', but instead, she demonstrated her interest by following up on what Jake was saying: 'It sounds like it was fun, Jake … and what happened then? … You've really thought lots about it haven't you?' … and so on.

In this way, children are able to feel valued: 'I am worthwhile and important enough for you to stop and listen. You value my ideas.'

I need to like myself and to be honest about myself.

It is important for children to develop a sense of their *own* worth through their own self-assessment, not through the external judgement of adults. This internal sense of worth will be enhanced by the use of encouraging feedback rather than praise. You will be able to read more about this in the chapter on encouragement. Children feel a greater sense of self-esteem when they learn to evaluate themselves and to focus on how they feel about something, rather than on an adult's judgement.

'Well done' can mean from the adult's view something has been well completed according to their criteria, but how does the child feel about it?

Responsive adults will give feedback that enables children to focus on how *they* feel about what they're doing. For example, 'You look really pleased about finishing that puzzle, Sarah', makes it possible for the child to target her own feelings, rather than focus on how the adult feels about the puzzle being completed. In this way children will feel: I am okay as me and I can accept myself. I do not have to rely on someone else's judgement of me or my accomplishments.'

I *need to find my own positive, acceptable and special way of belonging.* As you will learn later in this book, we all need to feel we belong and are accepted. In fact, Alfred Adler, the founder of Individual Psychology, stated that: 'The basic motivation behind all social behaviour is the need to belong.'

Belonging is a basic human need. In order to develop effectively, children require this need to be met through a recognition of themselves as worthwhile people and an acknowledgement of their positive behaviours. Children gain a sense of belonging by being noticed, which of course can occur through positive or negative behaviour. These concepts are explored in later chapters on behaviour. It was stated at the beginning of this chapter that the responses children receive for their behaviour will influence not only their self-esteem, but also whether or not that behaviour continues to occur.

Adults need to give children feedback which enables them to be acknowledged and noticed for their positive behaviour thus enhancing their sense of belonging. Even the greeting at the door when children arrive gives them a sense of belonging and acceptance.

Children need to belong and it is the responsibility of adults to enable children to feel special just because they are who they are — for their own uniqueness. How often do we acknowledge to a child that we have noticed her? Adults need to recognise and acknowledge children to assist their sense of worth.

Anna, a 2½-year-old, was playing beside an infant, Tom. Tom grabbed Anna's wooden blocks and put them with his pile of toys in front of him. Instead of grabbing them back, Anna simply fetched some more blocks and said, 'You can have those ones this time, Tom.' Their Mum, Lina, saw this and normally would have taken no notice. However this time she said, 'Anna, thank you for letting Tom have those. It was thoughtful of you to get yourself some more.' In this way, Anna was being noticed for her positive behaviour and is forming a perception of 'belonging'. Of course it will not be fair on Anna if she is expected to always cooperate in this way.

Children's self-esteem will be enhanced and nurtured by adults who encourage this sense of worth, acceptance and competence.

The development of a self-esteem enhancing environment is like building a house. When you build a house, you need to firstly ensure the foundations are solid. Your self-esteem enhancing environment is your solid foundation. The basis for this foundation can be shown in the word SECRET:

S — **S**hared Responsibility
E — **E**quality
C — **C**ooperation
R — **R**espect
E — **E**ncouragement
T — **T**rust

A self-esteem enhancing atmosphere is a SECRET environment. These concepts are outlined in the following chapters and will form the foundation for effective relationships and a framework for understanding children's behaviour.

CHAPTER 1:
Review activities

1 Describe the two components of self-esteem.

2 Identify the major factors influencing self-esteem.

3 Describe the correlation between self-esteem and children's behaviour.

4 Identify the adult's role in the development of children's positive self-esteem.

Activities for further learning

1 Consider these two situations:
First, we are in a 2–3-year-old room in a child care centre. A child, Sarah, has a runny nose. Tom, the caregiver says, 'Oh, Sarah, your nose is running. Let's get the tissues.' He lets Sarah take a tissue from the box and encourages her to wipe her own nose. Tom then says, 'Thanks for doing that Sarah. Your nose will feel much better now.'

Later we see a different situation. The same child Sarah, has a runny nose. This time Helen, the caregiver, handles it slightly differently. Helen comes up to Sarah and says, 'Sarah, you've got a runny nose. I'll get a tissue.' So Helen reaches for the tissues and comes back to the sandpit where Sarah is. She says to Sarah, 'Hop up Sarah, I'm going to blow your nose. Come on, hop up.' Sarah stands up and puts her head back to have her nose wiped. 'Good girl,' says Helen, and Sarah moves away.

Now consider how these two children may respond differently to these approaches. What might have happened in situation 1, where Tom enabled Sarah to do something herself. What would it do to Sarah's sense of worth and competence?.

What do you think Situation 2 would do to Sarah's sense of worth and competence where Helen fetched the tissue for Sarah and wiped her nose?

In the first situation, Sarah came away grinning and commented to 3 or 4 other children, 'I blowed my nose!'

In the second situation, Sarah allowed her nose to be wiped and then just sat down again to play in the sandpit.

Make a comment on how Situation 2 could have been handled differently to enable Sarah to have a feeling of self-worth and competence.

2 Think about a time in your childhood when you felt accepted, when you felt confident, when you felt someone believed in you. Then write down three things about the way this person spoke to you, about their attitude towards you and what their body manner was like.

Now think back to a time in your childhood when you felt that someone didn't believe in you, didn't trust you or when you didn't feel accepted in the situation. Consider the same aspects, how did the person speak to you, what was their attitude towards you.

Describe how each situation made you feel. Think about why. Consider the implications of this for your interactions with children.

3 Consider the past few days with your children. Think of at least three times when you could have enhanced children's self-esteem by acknowledging their worth and their competence. Write down what you could have said or done in each situation.

Practise using these responses in future situations.

Recommended reading

Curry, Nancy & Johnson, Carl. *Beyond Self-Esteem: Developing a Genuine Sense of Human Value*, 1992, N.A.E.Y.C.

Dinkmeyer, Don & Losancy, Lewis. 1980. *The Encouragement Book*, Prentice Hall, N.J.

Satir, Virginia. *People Making*, London, Souvenir Press, 1987.

2

DEMOCRATIC RELATIONSHIPS AND EFFECTIVE GUIDANCE

After studying this chapter, the reader will be able to understand and describe appropriate methods of relating with infants, young children, co-workers and parents, based on respect, equality, trust, cooperation and responsibility.

It is essential for those working and interacting with young children to approach children's behaviour in a positive way. Individuals' personalities are formed in the first few years of life as they establish patterns of behaviour and self-esteem that will remain with them. Children are individuals with inherited personality characteristics, who as they mature and develop within their families acquire many different patterns of behaving.

They will try out and practice both acceptable and non-acceptable forms of behaviour. In doing this, they are learning about themselves and their world in order to establish their own unique behaviour patterns. The responses children receive to their various behaviours influence whether or not the behaviour continues. This, of course, means that persons interacting with young children need to be very aware of their own behaviour and reactions.

A democratic approach to caregiving

The need for children to establish acceptable behavioural patterns in society is indisputable. The manner in which this is achieved is critical to the child's well-being. The primary objective in democratic and effective guidance is to stimulate children into desirable ways of behaving, by using an approach based on the following five principles.

Social equality

Each person is equal in terms of human worth and dignity. Even though each individual has varying skills, knowledge and background, this does not make one person more worthwhile than another. A baby of 6-weeks is no less worthwhile a person than a grandmother of 60-years. Thus one individual is not seen as superior with others being inferior, but each is equal, no matter what their age, experiences or qualifications. This means that caregivers will regard children, parents and other adults as important as themselves in having a voice in making decisions or giving opinions. For example, the caregiver will value children's options and let them be involved in decisions such as: 'Shall we have morning tea inside or outside today?'

Children are not always able to have a say because of limited experience, but the belief in their worth is still there. The caregiver will use warm, open body language, such as a hug or smile, and be physically at the children's level whenever possible to let infants and young children know they are accepted.

Mutual respect

Mutual respect involves a two-way relationship between caregivers and other adults, between children and other children, and between adults and children. Each person will accept the other for who and what they are, and will show understanding of the other's beliefs and values, even if not agreeing. It really means treating babies, children and other adults in as sensitive a manner as you would wish to be treated yourself. Caregivers showing respect will be aware of other's feelings and will be careful to avoid sarcasm or revenge.

The caregiver will be at the children's level whenever possible

It is especially important to consider how respect and equality for babies will be shown, as they are often treated with little regard for their feelings of worth. For example, a respectful caregiver will talk calmly and sensitively with a baby before changing her nappy or wiping her nose. The caregiver will then carry out the activity in a gentle and caring manner, talking about what is being done and why. Perhaps this takes a few seconds more of the caregiver's time, but babies and young children have a right to respect. Through being handled in this manner young children will imitate, and will themselves demonstrate respectful behaviour with peers and caregivers, creating an atmosphere of mutual respect.

Trust

Trust will be shown between adults who will, in turn, trust children for who and what they are. This will give the children a basis to have the courage to grow and develop positive attitudes toward themselves and others. Trust in each other is necessary in a secure, democratic environment where limits are fair and reliable.

Children and parents trust that caregivers will use their experience and knowledge to provide a quality, secure environment, and caregivers trust children to interact appropriately within that environment. In order to feel okay about themselves and others, children need to believe that they are trustworthy and that adults are reliable and dependable.

For example, a father who returns to the Centre at about the time the child is expecting him, or the caregiver who tells a young child, 'I'll be there when I've changed Sophie's nappy,' and makes sure she follows through with this, are both enabling children to develop feelings of trust in other people.

Cooperation

This involves modelling a cooperative attitude. It means working together with other adults to assist one another, and being willing to cooperate and be flexible with children so that each benefits by being with the others. People wishing to cooperate believe that the needs of others are as important as their own in working towards harmonious solutions. Cooperation demonstrates a willingness to share in an unselfish manner, so that all may benefit.

Cooperative caregivers will be eager to work on problems together, rather than believing that they have a greater or lesser share than another. Children sense this attitude and observe the behaviour, imitating it in both imaginative and real situations.

Caregivers demonstrating this approach will encourage children to work together on activities and jointly solve problems relevant to their abilities. However, it does not simply mean 'learning to share'.

For example, it may be a clear, sunny day and the caregivers and children have together decided (as an example of 'equality') that the morning snack will be taken outside. To encourage cooperation the caregiver may ask: 'What can you each do so that it is easier for us to have morning tea outside?' The children will be able to work together for the enjoyment of all.

Shared responsibility

Each person (adult or child) has opportunities to contribute and to show responsibility appropriate to their stage of development. Being given responsibility helps children feel they belong and are accepted, because their contribution is needed to allow for effective functioning of the group or family. Shared responsibility enables young children to make some decisions about how and what they will contribute, or what role they will have, giving freedom of choice within secure, fair limits.

As has already been outlined, young children and babies are equally worthwhile as people as are older children and adults, yet adults have experience and knowledge which holds them responsible for many things. However, this does not mean that children cannot contribute or be answerable for some things according to their abilities and understanding. Shared responsibility means that children cooperate and are trusted.

For example, democratic caregivers will encourage children's participation in many of the daily routines such as table setting, putting out beds, packing away and so on. Infants will be encouraged to cooperate in putting away play things through reciprocal interactions where the child puts one away and the caregiver puts one away, in turn. These are activities that help children feel they are needed and that their presence is acknowledged. These young children rightly believe that in this secure environment they are capable of being in control of their own behaviour.

Our society is moving towards these ideas as a general approach to living. There has been a change away from autocratic ways and autocratic people, where one individual or group dominates others taking all responsibility for decision making, to an acceptance of a democratic approach to human relationships. This is essential if we are to encourage children to become responsible, independent individuals with a positive self-concept.

A democratic approach to caregiving is not a permissive approach. It does not involve allowing children to do as they please, but gives them the opportunity to develop and contribute in a responsible way in an orderly setting.

It is based on the preceding five principles and is dependent upon having an effective and responsible leader to guide and encourage as shown in Figure 1.

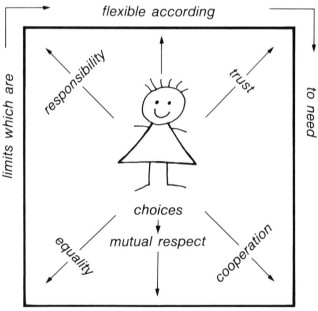

freedom with order = caregiver's responsibility

Figure 1 A democratic approach to caregiving

Effective caregivers will model these principles in their own behaviour and share them with children in a way that is appropriate to young children's development.

CHAPTER 2:
Review activities

1 Identify the five principles which form the basis of a democratic approach to relationships and effective guidance.

2 Describe how a democratic approach would differ from both permissive and autocratic approaches.

3 What role do significant adults (caregivers and parents) have in this approach?

Activities for further learning

1 Using the ideas presented in Chapter 2, identify at least two ways you might:
   (a) show respect
   (b) show trust
   (c) allow responsibility
   when interacting with children.

2 Establish three objectives for yourself in order to achieve a more democratic environment in your home or centre. Work towards these objectives in your daily routines.

3 Organise a parent information session with a speaker on Democratic Caregiving–Parenting where you discuss these ideas with parents and friends. Encourage parents to consider how they might translate the approach to their own parenting.

Recommended reading

Balson, M. *Becoming Better Parents*, Chapter 1.

3

AN INTRODUCTION TO PSYCHOLOGICAL PRINCIPLES

After studying this chapter, the reader will be able to identify the principles of Individual Psychology and Erikson's stages for understanding infant and child behaviour, especially as they relate to children's lifestyle perceptions.

Individual Psychology

The theory of Individual Psychology is based on the theories of Alfred Adler, a pioneer in personality development. It recognises people as active decision makers, as purposeful and goal-orientated individuals, relatively free to determine their own behaviour. The basic motivation behind all behaviour is the desire to belong, to be accepted and to contribute.

With this basic motivation in mind, behaviour should be viewed within the social setting. Children do not grow up in isolation. All behaviour such as language, play, emotion and skills are learned and developed in social situations such as the home, the day care centre, kindergarten and school. With this understanding, the caregiver can learn to respond appropriately in order to communicate with and guide children in a cooperative, respectful manner.

A child perceives herself as belonging according to the responses she has gained from the significant caregivers in her life. This will be discussed in more detail in Chapters 8 and 9 when we look at identifying and understanding the purposes of children's positive and negative behaviour. Even the most antisocial behaviour is an expression by children of their means of finding a place in the family or group. It is based on the mistaken or faulty belief that they cannot belong through constructive or acceptable means.

The effective caregiver will recognise the importance of children's sense of belonging and help children to feel good about themselves within the group or family. For example, the caregiver could greet each child or baby individually as they come into care, encourage (not praise) their acceptable behaviours and efforts, offer opportunities for each child to help in the program and with routines (table setting, saying names for going to the bathroom, choosing the story, picking flowers for vases), and show appreciation for their help.

Erikson's stages of development

Erikson (1963) in his book *Childhood and Society* outlined and discussed the development of socialisation and personality. He identified eight stages through which all normal human behaviour progresses, with the first three relating to the early childhood years.

Children develop in a predictable sequence of stages where a certain learned behaviour comes before another. Each of Erikson's stages is presented as the child's basic personality decision about their perception of themselves in their environment, which as individuals they resolve by observing and experiencing the world around them.

- *Infants:* in general terms are considered to be between the ages of newborn to approximately 18-months.
  Infancy is the time when a baby is establishing trust in people and the environment. Babies need to feel safe in a loving, nurturing situation where they know that if they are hungry, they will

Caregivers will show appreciation for children's help with routines

be fed; if they are lonely, they will be comforted; if they are in danger, they will be rescued. Babies are also learning to trust themselves and objects in their environment, so that they themselves may begin to pull their special blanket up to their face or to find comfort from their thumbs. *The infant is beginning to see her world as a friendly, trustworthy place.*

□ **Toddlers:** refers to children who normally are mobile and aged between about 18-months and 3-years.

A toddler is developing into an individual trying to gain independence and autonomy. Toddlers desire to do things on their own, for they have already learned to trust through the nurturing and love of infancy. Their sense of self is developing and they will insist on doing everything for themselves, although they may still be unsure of their skills and abilities. *The toddler is desiring independence but still wants someone secure there for her.*

□ **Preschoolers:** are usually considered to be between the ages of 3- to 5-years. (The term 'preschool' is an early childhood description which carries no implication that a child of this age is necessarily attending a preschool or any other program 'pre' a formal school education.)

A preschooler is becoming a creative and imaginative individual whose independence and trust now allows broader relationships and ideas. Imaginative play becomes very important to preschoolers because day-to-day situations can be acted out and they can imitate adults. Preschoolers need friends and really do desire to please the adults and children they care about. *The preschooler is beginning to learn of her independence and influence within her environment.*

Successful development through each of these stages in turn leads to the formation of a healthy person with a positive self-concept and lifestyle perception. It is important for the development of infant's and young children's positive feelings about themselves, their self-concept, and associated positive behaviours, that caregivers find appropriate ways to provide for these stages through interaction and play. Effective caregivers will have appropriate expectations for the social and emotional stages young children are in, and will respond accordingly. Through effective communication and sensitive guidance, the caregiver will stimulate children into desirable developmental and behavioural patterns. The caregiver will use methods based on *mutual respect, cooperation, trust, shared responsibility and social equality.*

Lifestyle perception

Each child develops a unique pattern of behaviour which becomes their personality and part of their lifestyle. To understand children we must be aware of their lifestyle perception and the factors which contribute to its formation.

Lifestyle is influenced by factors such as the child's desire to belong and the child's place in the family constellation, that is, the birth order of each child in the family.

The development of a unique style of life begins at birth as infants seek to understand their world and their relationship to it. Young children operate on a trial and error basis, evaluating each activity in terms of their own perception of its consequences. By the time children are about 5- or 6-years old, this lifestyle perception becomes stable. This then produces *their* interpretation of their relationship with their social environment. However, young children do not always see reality as it is and so draw incorrect conclusions. For example, an only child, Cindy, is told how fortunate she is because they are going to have a new baby, so she looks forward to playing, cuddling and so on. When the new baby arrives he takes up much of Mummy's time and always seems to be crying. Cindy tries to claim attention but begins to feel left out and may incorrectly believe that she is not valued as much as the new baby.

Mike, aged 5, always brings his drawings and paintings home from day care to show Daddy. Daddy picks out the recognisable 'good' work and makes a fuss of Mike for it. Mike gradually brings home less and less creative work because he believes that Daddy only values him when he produces 'good' work, and he cannot do that all the time. Mike may eventually develop a belief that he is only worthwhile when he can be the best.

We all need to feel we are recognised or that we count. The need is there at birth and the process of fulfilling that need begins immediately. In infancy, lifestyle beliefs begin to emerge through the process already outlined of trial and error of what works or what is valued in this particular family. This may lead to children within a family developing opposing characteristics and skills because of each one's desire to be recognised as special, and feeling unable to be accepted in areas where a brother or sister excels.

This typical family constellation with children showing opposing characteristics is represented in Figure 2.

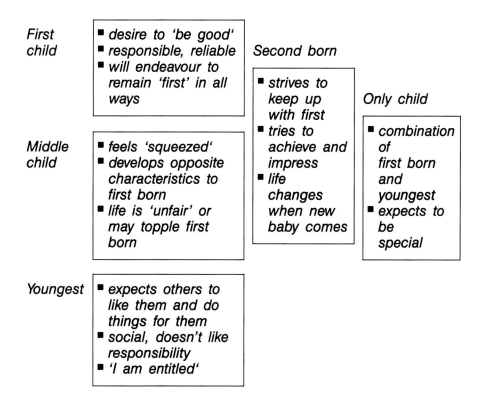

First child	▪ desire to 'be good' ▪ responsible, reliable ▪ will endeavour to remain 'first' in all ways	Second born

Second born

	▪ strives to keep up with first ▪ tries to achieve and impress ▪ life changes when new baby comes

Middle child — ▪ feels 'squeezed' ▪ develops opposite characteristics to first born ▪ life is 'unfair' or may topple first born

Only child — ▪ combination of first born and youngest ▪ expects to be special

Youngest — ▪ expects others to like them and do things for them ▪ social, doesn't like responsibility ▪ 'I am entitled'

Figure 2 A typical family constellation

As can be seen, children see themselves as belonging and being accepted in the family or group from their own personal perceptions developed from their experiences. The consequences of their lifestyle perception for some children is that they believe they are only acknowledged when displaying certain behaviours that have been reinforced or rewarded, giving them a sense of belonging. Acceptable and unacceptable behaviours which offer children a feeling of importance, recognition and belonging will be continued even though unacceptable behaviours are usually punished. Once a lifestyle pattern begins to develop, infants and young children will cease to act randomly and their behaviour can be related to achieving a sense of belonging in either a positive or negative way.

In our society, certain lifestyles are common and children's behaviour can be broadly categorised as follows:

□ *Contribution:* wanting to contribute and be involved in the group
□ *Responsibility:* being willing to accept responsibility and autonomy
□ *Cooperation:* interested in cooperating and being fair with others in the group.

The above behaviours indicate that the child feels she belongs and is recognised for her positive behaviours. These behaviours are reinforced and encouraged so she has no need for developing consistent patterns of misbehaviour.

A categorisation of negative behaviours is:

□ *Attention:* seeking to keep people busy with inappropriate attention
□ *Power:* wanting to be in control and superior or bossy in relationships
□ *Revenge:* needing to hurt or get back at others.
□ *Assumed inadequacy:* assuming an attitude of being unable or incapable.

Consistent behaviours such as these indicate that children have developed mistaken ideas about their lifestyles in gaining recognition for misbehaviour and negative actions.

In Chapter 8: 'Understanding the purposes of behaviour', readers will be able to identify which behaviours children are showing, and learn appropriate responses to encourage children's positive lifestyle beliefs.

If you can help children toward this, you will have achieved an incredibly important function. You will have contributed towards the development of responsible and reliable individuals, who have good feelings about themselves, who trust others around them, and who are able to function effectively in cooperative social relationships.

Infants and young children do *want* and *need* you to like them, to respect them, to encourage them and to recognise them as an accepted member of your group or family.

CHAPTER 3:
Review activities

1 Explain Adler's concept of the basic motivation behind behaviour.

2 Describe lifestyle perception and identify two factors which influence it.

3 Identify the four broad categories which can best describe purposes of negative behaviour.

4 Describe the personality issues of infants and young children as identified by Erikson for the period of development 0–6 years.

Activities for further learning

1 Consider your own schooldays and identify classmates who you believed received acknowledgement or recognition as belonging to a group through inappropriate behaviour, in terms of the four goals of negative behaviour. For instance, the 'class clown' may have felt she belonged by keeping others busy with her comic attention-seeking behaviour.

2 Identify your own family constellation and describe how you felt about your place in the family.

3 Discuss the concept of family constellation with a group of people, then divide the group into three according to their place in the family — eldest, middle, youngest.

Each small group is to identify at least five characteristics that apply to the upbringing of the people in that group, for example, responsible, spoilt, unfairly treated and so on. Return to the large group and share ideas. Consider how these ideas will apply to the children with whom you interact.

Recommended reading

Balson, M. *Becoming Better Parents*, Chapter 2.
Dinkmeyer, D., McKay, G. & Dinkmeyer, J. *Parenting Young Children*, Chapter 1.
Erikson, E.H. *Childhood and Society*, Chapter 2.

■ SECTION I ■

UNDERSTANDING CHILDREN: A NEW APPROACH

Summary

Changing patterns in society are creating feelings of apprehension for some of those involved in the care of infants and young children. The traditional autocratic system where one individual or group is superior to another is no longer appropriate, yet many adults wanting to effectively guide young children are unsure as to what approach they should use. A democratic framework for human relationships offers an effective and sensitive approach based on the values of equality, mutual respect, cooperation, trust and shared responsibility.

The basic motivation associated with all social behaviour is the need to belong, to be accepted and to contribute. Young children are establishing patterns of behaviour based on this motivation and the responses they receive from the people around them. Children's behaviour is influenced by their perceptions about their lifestyles, particularly their interpretation of belonging within a group or family, and their place in the family constellation. Young children want to be noticed and will develop both acceptable behaviours and associated beliefs to enable achievement of their goal. Responsive caregivers will recognise these various lifestyle beliefs and learn to appropriately reinforce positive beliefs and acceptable behaviours.

Adults, who show a sensitive understanding of children together with a democratic approach to caregiving, provide young children with the opportunity to develop in positive ways within a secure environment. This encourages children towards responsible and independent behaviour.

■ *S E C T I O N I I* ■

DEVELOPING POSITIVE RELATIONSHIPS

Focus

It will come as no surprise to readers to hear that a variety of investigations have found that attentive, warm, stimulating care-giving, that is responsive to children's needs and stages of development, facilitates the positive growth of children's self-esteem and feelings of acceptance.

4

*E*NCOURAGEMENT

Encouragement is the most self-esteem enhancing tool a responsive caregiver can have. Used appropriately, encouragement enhances self-esteem and prosocial behaviour. It focuses on the child rather than the adult. Encouragement conveys respect and acceptance. It helps children feel that the adult is interested in them and that the adult has taken time to notice what they are doing or how they are feeling.

Encouragement is an important aspect in the development of cooperative and contributive attitudes in children. It feels satisfying to a child to have somebody making a comment or showing an interest in what the child is doing, rather than just making statements of 'Good girl' or 'Good boy' after the child has achieved something. Encouragement is different from praise, as praise implies judgement or reward. It can be difficult to implement encouraging language because we have been raised with praise ourselves. However, children will develop a more positive sense of self-worth through having encouragement used so it is important to change one's focus from praise to encouragement.

Children who are only used to praise may become dependent on it. In other words, they may feel, 'I am only worthwhile when you are telling me I'm good or that something I've done is well done.' Young children who rely on praise in order to feel accepted will continue in this manner throughout their lives and thus may become very dependent on other people's judgement of their worth rather than developing a sense of 'I believe I am OK'.

Praise is very much an adult judgement. Praise depends upon an adult saying, 'You are doing it the way I think you should do it.' Praise can be a type of reward given by an adult. Because it is an external reward, rather than an intrinsic motivation, praise always depends on someone else telling the child they are good or they are accepted. This may well lead to peer group problems in adolescent years as young people will desire their peers' acceptance. As responsive caregivers we need to encourage children to feel comfortable and accepted with themselves. Children need to make their own judgements of self-worth and not be dependent on another person to make those judgements. A feeling of being a worthwhile and unique person comes from adults accepting the child as she is, not from adults judging the child on her performance and her achievements. Children believe the messages that adults either state or non-verbally convey to them. They need feedback, not judgement from adults.

Responsive adults will use encouragement to assist children's feelings of self-worth and acceptance by focusing on actual observations, rather than inferences, of what the child is doing, how she seems to be feeling and what her needs may be.

For example, a child who is doing a construction that is particularly difficult may look like he is going to give up. As a responsive caregiver you will not say, 'Well done' because it is not completed, nor do you want to make that sort of judgement. However you can say, 'Wow, Theo, I can see you are working really hard at that construction. Look you've finished doing one side already.'

As mentioned earlier, it can be difficult changing our own language from praise to encouragement so maybe you would like to try some of these phrases for a start.

Caregivers will take time to notice what children are doing and how they are feeling

Phrases to try

Phrases that express achievement or difficulty
- Wow, you did it all by yourself.
- It looks like you've worked really hard on that.
- You've nearly finished.
- You looked so pleased.
- You're nearly there, you can do it.
- I bet it feels good to have done it all by yourself. How do you feel about it?
- I really enjoy listening to you reading.
- Gee, you've put a lot of thought into that.
- It looks like you're feeling really disappointed. How about we talk?
- Seems like you're really mad because it won't go right.
- Looks like you're feeling really happy about your teacher's comments.
- You've been concentrating there for so long. It looks like you're really enjoying it.
- It looks like you don't feel like staying there for long and you want to go on to something else.
- You look like you're feeling worried about those comments.

Phrases that are appropriate to use for independence and routine times like dressing, toileting and eating
- Look, you've nearly finished. You must have enjoyed that.
- I bet it feels good to have done it by yourself.
- You looked so pleased about your new clothes.
- Wow, You went to the toilet all by yourself.
- You kept your nappy dry, it looks like you're happy about that.
- You look really pleased about going to the toilet all by yourself.
- I can see you've dressed all by yourself.
- You look really happy about the way you've dressed yourself.
- You really enjoy dressing yourself, don't you?
- Looks like you were really hungry. You've eaten everything for lunch.
- You must have been feeling thirsty. You've finished your drink and are ready for another one.

Phrases that express appreciation for helping

- You've put everything back in it's right place. Thank you, that saves me from doing it.
- Wow, you've nearly finished doing that. You must be pleased.
- I bet it feels good to have done that yourself, rather than waiting for me to do it.
- That is pretty tricky, but I'm sure you can do it.
- Thanks for doing that, it really saves me time.
- We all really enjoyed that food you prepared.

Phrases to use with artwork or children's play activities

- You've mixed different colors to make a new color here. Would you like to tell me how you did it?
- Look at all the colors you've used in your painting.
- Look at the way you've put that onto your page.
- Seems like you're really mad because it won't go the way you want it to.
- It's quite difficult isn't it, but I'm sure you can do it.
- You've been concentrating there for so long. It looks like you're really enjoying doing that.
- Look at the way you've put those together. They're really staying on well.
- You must be pleased that you've worked it out so that they would stay on.

It is important that responsive caregivers be aware that showing encouragement may be as simple as the type of experiences they are providing for children. Adults need to accept that children are all different and each one needs a range of experiences from effortless to challenging. Then, children can try out their skills and feel comfortable about themselves in order to not feel discouraged.

Children need to develop their own initiative and understanding over many aspects of their lives. Their own individual exploration will lead them to feelings of self-awareness and acceptance of their own strengths and weaknesses. If you consider back to Chapter 1, you will remember that this is an important feature of positive self-esteem. Children do not need other people to focus on their weaknesses. They do need responsive adults who will appreciate, encourage and acknowledge them.

CHAPTER 4:
Review activities

1 Identify and describe the significant features of encouragement.

2 Describe the influence of encouragement on children's self-- esteem. Outline the effect it will have on their sense of worth and their sense of competence.

3 Read the following statement of praise and convert it to a phrase of encouragement. 'Good girl, Alysha! You've finished all your fruit.'

Activities for further learning

1 Consider a time in your childhood when you felt another person encouraged you. You probably felt they believed in you, and they focused on what you could do instead of what you couldn't do. Think about what this person did or said. As a child how did that make you feel? Write down three implications your experience may have for you as a responsive caregiver of young children.

2 Write an encouraging letter or note to another adult or a child recognising their positive behaviour and acknowledging their feelings.

3 Consider this situation. Ashleigh has been busy packing away the dough toys. On previous occasions it seems that Ashleigh deliberately avoids packing away but on this occasion she is assisting. The caregiver says to Ashleigh, 'Thank you for help- ing Ashleigh. The other children really appreciate you doing

some with them.' Ashleigh responded, 'Yes, I put the rolling pins away and I cleaned the table.' The next day when the dough toys were out and it was time to put it away, the caregiver noticed that Ashleigh initiated the packing away process herself.

Describe the process of encouragement being used in this case study.

What consequence did encouragement have for Ashleigh, the other children and the caregiver?

Consider Ashleigh's possible responses if the statement of praise such as 'Good girl' had been used instead of encouragement. Include in your discussion the effect a statement of praise may have had on Ashleigh's self-esteem and on her sense of competence.

EFFECTIVE RELATIONSHIPS WITH INFANTS

After studying this chapter, readers will be able to apply the principles of Individual Psychology and democratic relationships to their interactions with infants and toddlers.

Infants need a caregiver who is available for comfort and play, to assist with feeding and changing, and to provide reassurance when security is needed. Infants who feel they are essentially accepted and recognised for their positive behaviours will grow up feeling acknowledged and okay about themselves. However, infants who are given the message that they 'are naughty' or 'a burden', or who receive more recognition for negative than positive behaviour, will grow up feeling discouraged and unsure of belonging through positive means. These infants soon develop a lifestyle perception about the way they are acknowledged based on negative responses and behaviour.

Infants need to believe in their environment and trust their caregivers to provide for their needs. Infants and toddlers have seesaw feelings between wanting to assert themselves and be independent of others, while doubting their own abilities. They need the security of a caregiver who can allow freedom with limits in a positive manner.

Very young children may know of no way to express a sense of identity, an 'I am me', other than say 'no' to adult direction. Understanding this, a caregiver can phrase directions or guidance in such a way that the child can begin to make her own choices and feel that she has direction and independence in positive ways. An infant in a caring relationship which allows her to experience some freedom within limits, in a trusting and respectful environment, will most likely become a secure cooperative child who feels okay about herself. It is the discouraged infant who may become the misbehaving child in order to feel she is recognised.

It is important to understand that adults cannot make infants or toddlers behave acceptably, so resorting to physical punishment or humiliation is never appropriate. Responses of this nature provide increasing rejection, discouragement and negativity in the child, thus providing neither a model of what is acceptable nor reinforcing positive behaviour. Adults can provide an environment and model behaviour where infants and toddlers can learn to limit themselves with positive guidance from caregivers. A responsive caregiver will respond to the very young child by developing her acceptable skills and attitudes, and extending her knowledge of the world, while still allowing her to be responsible for her own behaviour.

Psychological principles for very young children

The psychological principles which apply to understanding children's behaviour also apply when working with very young children.

1 Democratic relationships require trust, cooperation, respect, equality and shared responsibility

As has been discussed, infants need to believe in their caregiver's abilities to comfort, reassure and meet their needs, as this develops trust. However, it doesn't mean that the caregiver must drop everything she is doing the minute a baby cries — the relationship is one of cooperation and mutual respect. So that if the infant hears the caregiver's calm voice responding in a manner that gives the message: 'I can hear you, and it seems like you need something. I'll be there soon', then a trusting cooperative relationship is developed and continued.

The concept of respect is especially important. An adult's respect for infants and belief in individual equality of worth is an undeniable influence on the infant's future lifestyle perception, self-concept formation and relationships with others.

Respect means handling and treating the baby in a sensitive manner to indicate your care and affection for the infant. Infants deserve and have a right to be treated as we ourselves wish to be. Respect can be shown by talking, touching and soothing.

Infants and toddlers should be allowed to be who and what they want to be, within a secure environment with fair limits. In this way you are showing respect and trust in them as individuals, not trying to force them to be what you want.

A baby is shown respect by allowing her time for uninterrupted play and exploration. It is too easy to interrupt babies and just pick them up without a word to change their nappies, wipe their noses and so on. It is appropriate to talk with infants and prepare them for different experiences and routines as you would a toddler or preschooler.

A baby has every right to be treated and handled in the same way one would a child who can tell you what she does and doesn't like. What *you* can do is convey a responsive message of respect and sensitivity through your voice and manner. It is known that babies comprehend and understand much more than they can communicate, so this can be used to develop an effective and caring relationship.

2 Encouragement of infants

Encouragement comes in the form of body language *and* verbal communication. Caregivers can respond to infants in a warm manner that is expressed through voice, facial expression and body language. An infant's good feelings about self are nurtured with gentle voices that can be firm yet caring, and with appreciative looks that show interest and acceptance. If we accept that the discouraged infant becomes the misbehaving child, then the

A baby is shown respect by allowing her time for uninterrupted play and exploration

notion of adult encouragement of children beginning from birth is essential.

Caregivers can use natural voices and interesting language to encourage infants in their positive behaviours, and to provide calm and sensitive environments. Talk which is 'baby talk' is unnecessary and simply reinforces a superior–inferior concept. It provides neither appropriate language modelling nor a respect for individual equality. Infants do not need words to be babied, they need to hear natural language used in a simple appropriate manner.

Caregivers can further encourage the infant's development of positive self-concept and acceptable lifestyle perception by using positive communication. So instead of using 'no' or 'don't' constantly, the caregiver can let the baby know what she *can* do. For example, 'Let's pick you up and put you over here with these wooden pegs', instead of 'Don't touch the textas'. Positive communication with infants may also be non-verbal — just calmly and respectfully pick the child up and *do* something.

The responsibility rests with the caregiver to provide an environment appropriate to the infant's stage of development. It should allow her the opportunities for safe exploration without discouragement and feelings of inadequacy. She requires experiences that are challenging yet achievable, with a caregiver who allows her to be independent, but is there when needed. This is discussed in more detail in Chapter 13: 'Age-appropriate planning'.

Infants need to feel *they* are understood and accepted, even when their behaviour is unacceptable. Caregivers can encourage infants into acceptable expression of feelings by showing they understand and by offering alternatives. A*cknowledging* the feeling the infant has helps her to express and accept her feelings. For example 'It seems like you're feeling really frustrated Sarah . . . come and play with the warm water.'

This is discussed fully in Chapter 7: 'Responsive communication skills'.

Infants very early in life begin to perceive how they belong and gain recognition within a family or group. Hence the importance and use of encouragement, reinforcement and positive communication to help children develop good feelings about themselves.

3 Responsibility — freedom with order

During infancy and toddlerhood in particular, individuals need limits in order to feel secure, to develop trust in people and their environment, and to be safe. Consequently, the democratic approach is appropriate and effective as it allows individuals to have freedom while maintaining limits, and encourages them to begin accepting responsibility for their own behaviour. Again, positive communication is so important as it lets the infant know what she *can* do, what behaviour *is* acceptable, where she *can* do it, and so on. For example when Ahmad is grabbing the wooden pegs to poke Joel in the face, let Ahmad know where and how he can use the pegs by gently but firmly talking to him, and demonstrating how to use them. If he chooses not to use them acceptably, then he may either be offered an alternative piece of equipment or moved to another activity. It is usually necessary for caregivers of infants to physically maintain limits by either moving children, equipment or themselves, because infants have not yet developed skills of responsible behaviour, sharing and understanding consequences.

4 Purposes of behaviour — family constellation

Even young babies' behaviour is purposive, although a baby who won't sleep without being nursed may not necessarily be misbehaving, but may be expressing a survival need, for example a wet nappy, hunger, frustration and so on.

However, as babies mature and learn how they fit into a family or group, the purpose of their behaviour is influenced by their lifestyle perceptions and the response gained from those around them.

As discussed in Chapter 3, the child's place in the family will influence that child's lifestyle perception, so she will come into your care with particular beliefs about herself already formed. The first born or only infant may have many more pressures placed upon her with subsequent expectations of a 'wonderchild', than subsequent children in the family. The last born infant may remain immature and dependent because of family beliefs about wanting the youngest to remain 'the baby', and with older siblings to meet her every need, the infant also comes to believe that this is her 'place'. The middle child, who once held the privileged position of being the youngest, may feel pushed out and rejected by the new infant who has now made her a 'middle'.

Consideration needs to be given to infants' lifestyle perceptions, because their behaviour will develop into purposive patterns for belonging within a group, based in part on their perceived place in the family. Effective caregivers will respond with encouragement and respect, using appropriate guidelines for infant behaviour.

Responsive relationships based on trust, respect, knowledge and sensitivity, with a belief in the equal worth of infants, are what is required for responsible and effective caregiving to infants and toddlers.

CHAPTER 5:
Review activities

1 Identify three characteristics of social and personality development which need to be provided for in responsible and sensitive caregiving of infants.

2 Outline the psychological principles which apply to developing effective relationships with infants.

3 Describe two ways a caregiver can use encouragement to help an infant develop feelings of positive self-esteem.

4 Describe the influence that the family constellation may have on an infant's lifestyle perception.

Activities for further learning

1 Imagine you are in charge of a room with five babies. Two 10-month-old babies are occupied at an activity on the floor

but you need to change their nappies. How can you do this in a democratic manner which shows *respect* for their needs and feelings?

2 Practise using *positive* verbal and non-verbal communication with babies. Let them know what they can do, how they can do it, where they can do it, and so on.

3 Imagine a parent has just said goodbye and left the centre, and their infant is showing signs of being upset. Identify how you could acknowledge the child's feelings, both through gentle talk and physical contact.

CHAPTER

6

EFFECTIVE RELATIONSHIPS WITH YOUNG CHILDREN

After studying this chapter, the reader will be able to understand and identify appropriate techniques to further develop the young child's positive self-concept especially through the use of encouragement and positive communication.

When discussing effective relationships it is necessary to return to the principles of Individual Psychology which were outlined in Section 1.

The concepts of mutual respect, equality, choice, cooperation, acceptance and responsibility are all necessary to develop effective and trusting democratic relationships. These allow children to become independent young people with a positive view of themselves and life, able to contribute to their world around them.

As mentioned in Chapter 3, the preschool child is in Erikson's third stage of social–emotional development, where her individual personality is becoming more pronounced with complex feelings emerging. Her behaviour is very purposeful, investigative and independent, requiring an encouraging and stimulating environment.

The preschooler needs to be allowed opportunities to develop her creativity, independence and socialisation. She likes to take turns and share, and is beginning to care about other children's opinions. She gradually learns what is acceptable through acting out many situations in imaginative or dramatic play. She is concerned about adult acceptance, adult approval and receiving attention, in order to obtain the reassurance that she is still loved and still belongs.

Feelings are particularly important during the preschool years as children's emotions are developing and becoming more specific. Young children need to know that they are accepted and respected even though they may be having hurtful or angry feelings. This will be discussed, and appropriate caregiving skills to use in response will be described in Chapter 7: 'Responsive communication skills'.

Showing acceptance of children

The relationships young children form with adults during this period of development serve as a foundation for positive behaviour and strong self-esteem. Preschoolers need to feel good about themselves in order to respect others and behave in socially accepted ways. In other words an 'I'm okay — you're okay' position is important. Children who feel loved and accepted for who and what they are, are more likely to trust and accept other people, thus developing positive relationships.

Children who have received messages of 'You're not okay' from caregivers and others around them, may believe they are not acceptable as they are now. These children will feel discouraged and may attempt to gain recognition through negative behaviour.

For instance, Jackie may misbehave at times but still knows she is accepted and appreciated by the significant people around her. She will thus develop self-respect and self-acceptance, with her cooperation and respect towards others reflecting this attitude. By comparison Debbie, who also misbehaves at times, has received messages from the significant people in her life that she will only be valued and accepted when she becomes different. Debbie will find it difficult to be positive in her attitudes and cooperative towards others.

Balson (p.71) tells of the importance of accepting children for who and what they are. While all children are capable of improvement with practice, to focus on deficiencies is inappropriate and has a negative compounding effect on a child or adult.

Consider how you would feel if someone conveyed to you the message that you are not valued and, as you are, you are not good enough. Unless you are very sure of yourself you are likely to feel even less capable and worthwhile, thus becoming discouraged and lacking belief in your own self (see Figure 3).

Discouraged children may feel that they just cannot be good enough to be accepted by an adult or group. They may lose faith in their ability to cope with the demands of various situations, and will often feel inadequate, and so turn to negative behaviour. It should be remembered that the basic motivation behind all behaviour is the desire to belong, to be accepted and to be recognised.

A democratic caregiver will develop a relationship with the preschooler which is based on mutual respect, trust and a belief in each individual's equal worth. Young children need to be appreciated, encouraged and acknowledged in order to feel accepted and comfortable with themselves. The child who is warmly welcomed as she comes in the door by a responsive caregiver will feel noticed, worthwhile and okay about her place in the group.

To develop and improve warm and responsive relationships with children you need to convey a number of things. As described in Chapter 5, you can do this through your whole caregiving approach which will let children know you enjoy being with them. As much as possible you need to be at their level by squatting, kneeling or sitting down. You need to come to know your children as individuals, each with their own special values and needs. An adult who combines warmth, caring and freedom within fair and acceptable limits provides an appropriate model for effective relationships.

Responsive caregivers will use quiet voices which will be calm, sensitive, reassuring, yet firm and sharp when necessary. Their

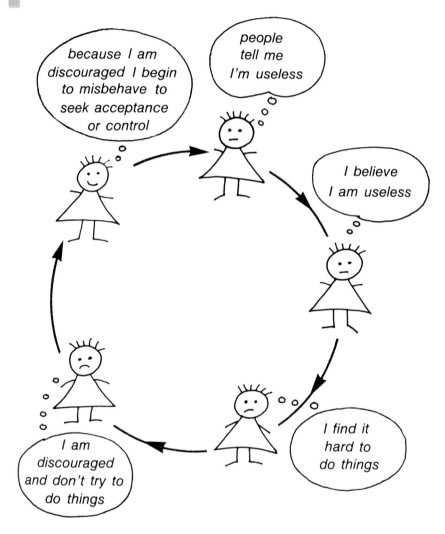

Figure 3 The cycle of discouragement

manner will be warm, open and accepting, with a willingness to have close contact with children at the children's own level whenever possible.

Through this warm, open manner and calm, reassuring voice, caregivers will convey respect, interest, care, acceptance, confidence and trust to their children. They can further extend this in a responsive environment through encouragement and positive guidance.

The caregiver's manner will be warm, open and accepting with a willingness to have close contact with children.

Encouragement of children

Encouragement focuses on the child's effort or process in doing something, and positive guidance focuses on what the child can do or is doing that is appropriate.

Encouragement is aimed at helping children feel good about themselves so that they develop positive self-esteem. It can and should be used at all times, and is critically important to use in instances when children don't feel on top of things. There is always something positive to encourage, a strength shown, an improvement made, or an effort in an attempt. Encouragement is given for effort and improvement, and focuses on what is being done rather than on the end product. It relies on how the child feels about the process rather than only what is achieved at the end, although it may do both.

For example, after Carlo has helped pack away his toys: 'Carlo, you really put lots of toys away then. It certainly is easier when we can help each other. Thank you.'

Perhaps when Stefan comes and asks you if you like his painting, you could say: 'It sure looks like you have enjoyed using the red paint today, Stefan' or 'How do *you* feel about it Stefan?'

Dinkmeyer and McKay (p. 33) describe encouragement as a 'focus on the assets and strengths of children in order to build their confidence and self esteem'. Encouragement is an important aspect of the development of a cooperative and contributive attitude in children.

We have to be very careful to distinguish *encouragement* from *praise* as each has a different purpose.

Praise can be seen as a type of reward given by an approving adult. It is an attempt to motivate children by external rewards or values such as 'you are so *good*' . . . or 'so *pretty* . . . or 'I'm very *proud* of you'. It focuses on the end product rather than on how the child feels about something. Praise can become discouraging and very hard to live up to. For example, children may become concerned as to whether they can always 'be that good', 'be that pretty', or 'do that well'.

Praise develops a competitive drive in children and makes them want to be the best in order to win approval. So when Nikita finishes her puzzle instead of saying, 'Good girl', it would be encouraging to say: 'It looks like you really enjoyed doing that puzzle today, Nikita'.

It is important to remember that children who are encouraged and feel good about themselves can and do excel, but in a cooperative way rather than at the expense of others. Encouragement is particularly valuable for the over-ambitious child who is desiring to be better than all others and so may set impossibly high goals for herself. Often these children don't finish things because they assume that they cannot do them as perfectly as they think they should, and they may not turn out to be better than everyone else's after all.

Using positive guidance

As was stated at the beginning of this chapter, one of the aims of the responsible caregiver should be to help young children develop a positive self-concept, and to feel accepted for who and what they are.

The skill of using positive guidance to develop effective relationships with young children expands the growth of children's positive self-esteem. Caregivers will let children know what is acceptable and what they can do, rather than focusing on what they cannot do (see Figure 4). For example, instead of saying:

'don't run inside', say

'remember to walk inside'

'don't splash the water', say

'the water should stay in the trough'

'your shoes are on the wrong feet', say

'I see you've put your shoes on by yourself',

thus focusing on the positive part of the act.

Figure 4   The caregiver will show appreciation for the positive aspects of a child's behaviour

The effect of concentrating on mistakes is to reinforce the child's belief that she is incapable or not good enough, and so continues the cycle of discouragement outlined in Figure 3. We can become so used to criticising children that we actually reinforce inappropriate behaviour by drawing attention to it and then, because this gives recognition, children will repeat it. Caregivers need to centre attention on the things children can do and appreciate them.

Responsive and effective caregivers let children know they are appreciated and accepted. They will focus on strengths, recognise efforts, and minimise dwelling on mistakes or insufficiently developed skills.

CHAPTER 6:
Review activities

1 Outline the democratic values which are essential to responsive and effective relationships with young children. (These were explained more fully in Chapter 5.)

2 Identify why it is particularly important for children in the preschool years to feel accepted and to be comfortable with themselves.

3 Describe the effects of discouragement on young children.

4 Define and explain what is meant by encouragement.

5 Outline why caregivers should use positive guidance with young children.

Activities for further learning

1 Compose an *encouraging* response to each of the following situations. Remember to focus on how children feel about themselves and what they are doing.
   (a) A 3-year-old dresses herself with her jumper back to front, shoes on the wrong feet and socks inside out.
   (b) A 5-year-old helps you pack away but puts things in the wrong place.

(c) An 18-month-old has just used the toilet and her nappy has been dry for hours.

2 Write down and learn some phrases of encouragement to use at appropriate times with your children.

3 Identify situations where you would normally use praise with children. Now write down and use alternative responses which are encouraging and foster positive self-esteem.

Recommended reading

Balson, M. *Becoming Better Parents*, Chapter 5.

Dinkmeyer, D. & McKay, G. *Systematic Training for Effective Parenting: Parent's Handbook*, Chapter 3.

Dinkmeyer, D., McKay, G. & Dinkmeyer, J. *Parenting Young Children*, Chapter 3.

7

RESPONSIVE COMMUNICATION SKILLS

After studying this chapter, the reader will be able to identify and use responsive verbal and non-verbal communication skills by recognising the importance of encouragement, reflective listening and 'I' messages to acknowledge and express feelings.

In Chapters 5 and 6, 'Effective relationships with infants' and 'Effective relationships with young children', it was said that the concepts of mutual respect, equality, freedom of choice, cooperation, acceptance and responsibility, are all necessary in order to develop effective and trusting democratic relationships. However, to *maintain* a satisfying relationship with your children you need to be able to communicate effectively with them, both in talking and in listening, and so demonstrate mutual respect. This means that both children and adults will allow each other to express their feelings honestly without fear of rejection or disapproval.

Communicating with children

When adults and young children communicate in this way, both will develop 'good' feelings about themselves, and children will feel valued and accepted with a high level of self-esteem. Responsive caregivers will use effective communication, talking about what children are able to do, and recognising the efforts they are making. Effective communication is honest, is not condescending to children, and is sensitive, acknowledging that it is not necessary to say everything that may be thought or felt. It is important that the caregiver's tone of voice is pleasant and expressive, reflecting friendliness and interest in young children. Children need to be given time to 'talk back' with adults who follow up their conversation, thus helping children feel worthwhile and accepted.

For instance, when Sammy comes to the early childhood centre on Monday morning he may tell the caregiver, 'I went to Nanna's yesterday night'. A response could be: 'Did you?' However that does not indicate interest or acceptance, it merely closes the conversation. A sensitive and interested response would be: 'It sounds like it was night-time when you were at Nanna's. Did you have tea there Sammy?', and so the conversation would progress. It may even continue with the caregiver telling Sammy what *she* had for tea. For example, Sammy may have responded 'Yes, we had yummy chicken and chips for tea'. The caregiver's reply could then have been: 'It sounds like you really enjoyed your tea. I enjoyed my tea also. I had cheese on toast last night. Do you ever have that Sammy?'

As you can see, Sammy will feel accepted and worthwhile through this caregiver showing genuine interest, giving him time and attention.

Positive and responsive communication will also occur through non-verbal behaviour using a warm, open, accepting manner and respectful body language.

As so much communication is non-verbal, caregivers need to be very aware of their manner with young children. Open body language is demonstrated when caregivers position themselves at the children's or babies' level and maintain eye contact, when they are relaxed and warm in their approach, when they are smiling not only with their mouth but also with their eyes, and when they are conveying the message 'I like being with you' to infants and children.

Through this warm, open manner and a calm, reassuring voice, caregivers can convey democratic values which will enhance effective communication. One way of doing this is through the process of encouragement which was discussed in Chapter 6.

Encouragement is a way of focusing on the child's effort or process of working towards something, in order to build the child's self-esteem and confidence. When encouragement is used it allows children to feel good about themselves and accepted, even when things don't go right. The caregiver will show *acceptance of children* even though their *behaviour* may not be appropriate. Encouragement is *not* the same as praise, as was shown in Chapter 6.

After continual praise, children may start to believe that their worth is dependent upon what others think of them, whereas encouragement helps a child become self-motivated. You may wish to reflect on the examples of encouragement given in Chapter 6 or consider the following situation.

When Joshua finishes his drink and the caregiver says: 'Good boy, Joshua', that is praise. It is focusing on the caregiver's perception of her value of Joshua, and does not help Joshua understand why you think he is 'good'. However, if the caregiver says: 'It looks like you really enjoyed that drink, Joshua', that is encouragement. It is focusing on Joshua's feelings and helps him clarify why the caregiver is encouraging.

Just as in effective communication, words are not always necessary for children to feel encouragement, touch is also important. For instance, a reassuring cuddle, a pat on the shoulder or a smile of acceptance all help children to feel valued for who and what they are.

Allowing children to express feelings

Self-concept is influenced by how we feel about ourselves and our beliefs. All humans have feelings and emotions, each person develops their own beliefs and values about acceptable and non-

Caregivers can convey the message 'I like being with you' to infants and young children

acceptable emotions. These beliefs are greatly dependent on parental or significant caregiver values. Thus children's acceptance and understanding of emotions will be influenced by what has been approved or disapproved of in their upbringing.

Feelings are real and a part of being human. Through appropriate communication, caregivers will learn to help children acknowledge how they feel and teach them appropriate ways to express feelings.

Children need freedom to express both their positive and negative feelings. Sharing positive feelings such as joy, pleasure, contentment and happiness enriches relationships. Learning to appropriately express negative feelings such as anger, hate, jealousy and revenge is an important social skill. Sometimes feelings seem so strong that people want to push them aside, but feelings are emotions that need to be understood, accepted and appropriately expressed.

It is important for a child's mental health that she learns that it is okay to have feelings. For instance, for a long time the right to feel pain and sadness seemed to be reserved only for females. This is changing along with the changing society we discussed in Chapter 2. Other examples of changing ideas that are now seen as more acceptable are boys being able to express sorrow and girls to express anger.

It is good to express feelings and get them out into the open. We need to help children acknowledge their feelings in an appropriate way. We can do this by effectively and sensitively listening to children, then *reflecting* back to them the feeling we think they are verbally or non-verbally expressing. For example, a *reflective statement* might be: 'Jono, it seems like you're feeling really mad with Tom because you wanted to sit there', when Jono bites and pushes Tom from the chair he wanted. To simply say: 'Jono, don't bite Tom' indicates little understanding of Jono's feelings.

Reflective listening acknowledges that it's okay to have the feeling and acknowledges the problem.

Even though we may acknowledge to the child that it is okay to have the feeling, we need to teach appropriate ways to channel that feeling.

For instance, using the above example: 'It seems like you're feeling mad with Tom because you wanted to sit there. That's okay, but you must not bite him. I would like you to come and use this lovely, soft clay. You can hit and squelch that.'

A further example: 'It seems like you're feeling really angry with me at bringing you inside right now, but I still will not allow you to hit me. Let's go and punch the punching ball instead.'

Children will feel understood when the *meaning* of their behaviour or language is acknowledged and accepted. Reflective listening needs to be expressed in a calm, encouraging manner, and is better if stated in a tentative way in case we're wrong about what or why the child is feeling. However, if you are unsure it is okay to make a guess about the feeling being expressed, as children will usually correct you if they believe you are genuinely sincere and accepting. For example, when Susie falls over in the playground, she grazes her knee and also breaks the arm from the doll she is carrying. A caregiver might cuddle her and say: 'Susie, it seems like you're feeling really sore from your hurt knee'. Susie's sobbing reply may indicate something different: 'No . . . (sob) . . . but I broke Tiffany's arm off . . . (sob)'. That gives a different direction for the caregiver's next reflective statement: 'You seem to be really unhappy about Tiffany's arm. Let's see what we can do'. Thus the caregiver will show acceptance and understanding whilst reassuring the child. Children who are listened to and receive these responsive messages come to feel valued and respected.

Reflective listening can also be used in the same way when children have a problem and come to you for help. For instance, a child using a frustrated voice says: 'These blocks just won't stay right'. A responsive caregiver will reply: 'It seems like you're really annoyed about those blocks. What do you think we can do about it?', thus acknowledging the child's feelings whilst encouraging responsibility and decision making.

Of course, an infant or toddler may simply express the above by throwing the blocks across the room. The same feelings are present, although very young children may be unable to identify their emotions. The caregiver's attitude, body language and tone of voice will best demonstrate acknowledgement and understanding. So, using a warm manner and positioning herself at the toddler's level, the caregiver may calmly say: 'It seems like you're feeling really frustrated with those blocks Lou, how about I find you some that will stack okay', and then stay close by to reassure and redirect if necessary.

As you can see, reflective listening can be used as an initiator to help children solve problems and explore alternatives. By using reflective listening you can encourage children to express and feel okay about emotions, and if appropriate, you can also involve them in working out a solution.

Children's fears should also be handled in this way. During the preschool years, in particular, young children express many fears and anxieties of their real and imaginary worlds. This fear is an emotion that should be acknowledged, however there is also some reality involved. For instance, it needs to be understood that the space under the bed is not inhabited by a dragon, but the child still needs reassurance. With adult guidance, children can learn to acknowledge and handle fears because they develop the intellectual capacity to accept reality. Be willing to offer calm, warm support without giving undue attention. For example, you may be out walking with children when they see a large dog across the road. One of the children, Daniel, stiffens and tightens his grip on your hand. You will:

1 acknowledge the fear

2 encourage the acceptance of reality

3 give reassurance.

So you may decide to squat at the children's level and say: 'Daniel, it seems like you're feeling frightened of that dog (step 1) . . . Yes, he is big isn't he . . . Yes, dogs do sometimes bite people, particularly if they hurt them . . . We need to keep walking so that we can go to the shop and buy some bread (step 2) . . . Let's have a cuddle and then we'll hold hands really tightly as we skip along' (step 3).

WORDS FOR REFLECTING

HAPPY FEELINGS	*UPSET FEELINGS*
accepted	*angry*
appreciated	*anxious*
capable	*defeated*
confident	*disappointed*
delighted	*discouraged*
encouraged	*embarassed*
excited	*frightened*
grateful	*hurt*
happy	*inadequate*
pleased	*miserable*
proud	*sad*
respected	*unhappy*
satisfied	*worried*

Figure 5 Feeling word list

If caregivers are to assist young children in feeling valued and respected, then it is important to use reflective listening techniques for both verbal and non-verbal behaviour. Children will gradually begin to understand their own and others emotions, modelling their behaviour on the responsive adults around them.

Figure 5 is a feeling word list to help you get started in identifying and acknowledging emotions.

Caregivers will be able to develop their own vocabulary list of words that they feel comfortable using. For more help refer to 'Activities for further learning' at the conclusion of this chapter.

Allowing caregivers to express feelings

So far we have discussed situations where *children* have problems and are expressing emotions, but consideration also needs to be given to *caregivers'* problems and feelings. Responsive caregivers will effectively and respectfully communicate their feelings to children, thus encouraging appropriate behaviours.

An example may be when children are using some new equipment inappropriately, causing concern or a problem for the caregiver, who may say: 'You shouldn't use it like that' or 'You should know better than that Polly'.

As was described earlier in this chapter, this sort of negative communication is discouraging and non-accepting. A more appropriate response is: 'When you bang the pieces together, I feel concerned because our equipment will be broken'.

This message is non-judgemental and does not lay blame, nor does it attack the child's self-esteem by saying she should know better. It is simply a calm statement expressing the caregiver's feelings about a particular behaviour. It *is called an* 'I' *message*.

In order to be most effective and understandable, an 'I' message has three parts:

1 describes the behaviour that is causing the problem, '*when you* bang the pieces together'
2 states the feeling that you have, 'I *feel* concerned'
3 outlines the consequences the behaviour may cause (or why you feel as you do), '*because* our equipment will be broken'.

When communicating with younger children it is more effective to simplify the 'I' message, while at the same time responding by intervening physically. For instance, in the above example the responsive caregiver would move the toddler away while saying: 'I'm concerned our equipment will be broken', and redirect the child's behaviour.

In Section IV, Chapter 10, there is more discussion on the use of 'I' messages as a guidance technique.

'I' messages are very effective means of communicating your own feelings to children, and are thus appropriate for positive as well as negative feelings. An 'I' statement can be very encouraging and appreciative. For example, 'I really appreciated you packing all the blocks away, Gino. It made cleaning up so much easier'.

Again, the three parts were used, but in different sequence:
1 states the feeling, 'I really appreciated'
2 describes the behaviour, 'you packing all the blocks away'
3 outlines the reasons, 'It made cleaning up so much easier'.

The sequence is not at all important, what is essential is that the message conveyed is genuine and respectful.

Children and adults need to be allowed to express feelings and be listened to without fear of being put down. When we communicate we convey our beliefs, values and respect for our children as individuals.

The communication skills that have been outlined are designed to enhance understanding between adults and children, thus encouraging positive relationships. With improved relationships, infants and children are more likely to behave appropriately. However, an encouraging manner, reflective listening and 'I' messages will need to be used *in conjunction with* the responsive guidance techniques outlined in Section IV.

CHAPTER 7:
Review activities

1 Outline three effective forms of communication which will enhance positive relationships and extend the democratic values described in Chapter 2.

2 Describe what is meant by 'feelings'. How can infants and young children be helped to accept them?

3 Describe how a responsive caregiver would handle children's expressions of fear or anxiety.

4 Outline the three parts of an appropriate statement expressing your feelings to children in a respectful manner.

Activities for further learning

1 Identify as many 'feelings' words as possible. Consider these and make a list of words which young children would understand.

2 Observe the behaviour of infants and young children, or even adults. Identify examples of non-verbal expression of feelings and decide on appropriate responses to *acknowledge* these feelings.

3 Respond to the following with a *reflective listening* statement:
   (a) A 5-year-old boy that you know sobs and says no-one wants to play with him.
   (b) A 3-year-old girl in your Centre screams at you when you remove her from the sandpit for repeatedly throwing sand.
   (c) A 2-year-old child greets you in the morning with a smiling face and enthusiasm.
   (d) A 10-month-old baby is crying when her parents walk out the door after saying goodbye.

4 Practice expressing *your* feelings through using 'I' *messages* for the following situations:
   (a) You come into the toilet and the whole roll of toilet paper has been unravelled into the toilet by a 2-year-old child.
   (b) You are telling a story to a group of 4-year-old children and one of them continually interrupts.
   (c) A 3-year-old child has just finished setting the tables for lunch.

5 Be ready to use positive communication skills whenever appropriate.

Recommended reading

Biddulph, S. *The Secret of Happy Children*, Chapter 3.
Dinkmeyer, D. & McKay, G. *Systematic Training for Effective Parenting: Parent's Handbook*, Chapter 4.
Dinkmeyer, D., McKay, G. & Dinkmeyer, J. *Parenting Young Children*, Chapter 4.

■ *SECTION II* ■

DEVELOPING POSITIVE RELATIONSHIPS

Summary

The democratic principles which apply to understanding children's behaviour may also be applied when developing positive and responsive relationships with infants and young children.

The concepts of respect and acceptance are especially important in reinforcing children's positive feelings of self-worth and trust in the significant people around them. Responsive caregivers will develop skills of encouragement and positive communication to help infants and children feel good about themselves, to prevent them becoming discouraged or feeling inadequate.

Infants are learning to trust those around them and discovering things about their world, some of which cause satisfaction and others, discomfort. Thus infants need a secure, trusting environment where their needs are met in a sensitive manner, in order that they may develop into toddlers who can form relationships and feel comfortable about themselves.

Toddlers are reaching out for independence from adults, yet still require adults nearby for security, limits and reassurance. These young children face many frustrations caused by their desires for exploration and independence, so positive relationships are enhanced through sensitive acknowledgement of problems.

Preschool age children also wish to do things for themselves and be independent. By now they have developed the creativity and initiative necessary for this. However, they have a desire to please adults, which sometimes causes them inner conflict. The responsive caregiver will show young children they are appreciated, accepted and worthwhile through using encouragement and positive communication.

Encouragement which acknowledges children's efforts, improvements and feelings should not be confused with praise or value judgements about children's work. Encouragement leads to cooperative and contributing children who feel good about themselves and those around them.

Responsive caregivers will use reflecting listening to acknowledge infants and children's feelings, and will encourage young children to express their feelings in appropriate ways. In the same way, when something is a problem to caregivers they may express their own feelings through using 'I' statements.

Effective and responsive listening and expression occurs through verbal and non-verbal communication with the caregiver's calm voice, warm manner and accepting body language being tremendously important.

■ S E C T I O N I I I ■

*U*NDERSTANDING CHILDREN'S BEHAVIOUR

Focus

In understanding young children, it is necessary that we have some knowledge of the psychological principles behind their behaviour. Most behaviour has a social purpose and is motivated by the need to belong, to be accepted, and to contribute. It is important that infants and young children feel they belong, and in these early years children will discover how to gain acceptance and recognition.

Children do not grow up in isolation. All behaviour, such as language, play, emotions and skills, is learned and developed in social situations like home, child care centres, kindergartens and schools. Their behaviour can best be explained when viewed within these social settings.

With this understanding caregivers can learn to respond appropriately in order to communicate with, and guide, children in a cooperative, respectful manner.

CHAPTER

8

UNDERSTANDING THE PURPOSES OF BEHAVIOUR

After studying this chapter, the reader will be able to under-stand children's behaviour in the context of their need to be recognised and accepted within their social environments. The reader will focus on children's positive behaviour, learning appropriate responses to reinforce it.

Individual Psychology recognises people as active decision makers, as purposeful and goal-oriented individuals, relatively free to deter-mine their own behaviour. Alfred Adler has said that the basic motivation behind all behaviour is the desire to belong, to be accepted, and to contribute. As outlined in Chapter 3 children perceive themselves as belonging according to the responses that they gain from significant caregivers at home, day care centre, family day care, kindergarten and school.

For instance, Jodie, aged 2½-years, has been in child care for 6 weeks and the caregivers have tried to help her feel comfort-able about her new surroundings. At times Jodie plays quietly and so is left alone by the adults. However most of the time Jodie whimpers and grizzles, so is picked up or given attention in some other way.

If we reflect on this situation from an Alderian viewpoint, it can be seen that Jodie's positive behaviour, her quiet play, is not gaining her any recognition, yet her negative behaviour of whimpering gains a response from the caregivers. Jodie's caregivers unintentionally ignore her positive behaviour, only taking notice of her and giving reassurance at negative times. *Responsive* caregivers will greet Jodie at the door then perhaps sit with her at activities for a short time, providing reassurance and comfort at times when Jodie is not demanding it. The caregiver may calmly and gently say, 'Jodie, it's really nice having you at our centre. It looks like you're enjoying sitting with Sam and me doing this puzzle'. This reinforces a positive belief that Jodie is able to belong and gain recognition through appropriate behaviours.

Not all behaviour is negative and not all children show inappropriate behaviours. When children feel loved, valued and respected, they love, value and respect themselves and other people in return. When children are discouraged, they are more likely to misbehave, so it is the caregiver's responsibility to encourage and respond to positive behaviour.

The goals of positive behaviour

Figure 6, Lifestyle perceptions — positive behaviour, illustrates how the basic social motivation of the desire to belong can be reinforced through children's positive and acceptable behaviour being encouraged by caregivers. Unfortunately, when children display acceptable behaviours such as sharing or helping, adults often take them for granted.

This figure shows how responsive caregivers will identify the child's belief about belonging, for example 'I belong by contributing', and recognise acceptable behaviour, for example 'helping; participating'. The caregiver will reinforce this behaviour through the approaches described, for example 'show appreciation of children's behaviour', thus facilitating the child's need for recognition through socially acceptable goals.

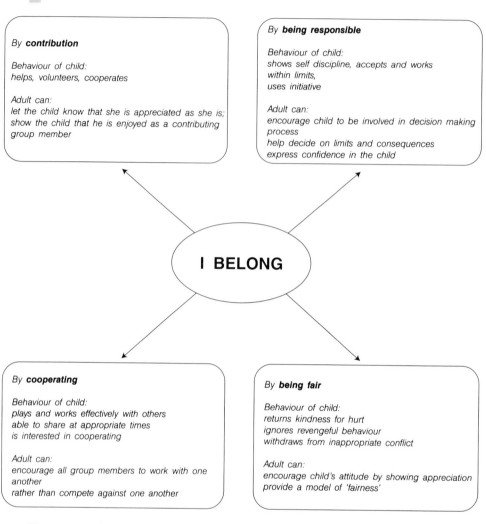

By **contribution**

Behaviour of child:
helps, volunteers, cooperates

Adult can:
let the child know that she is appreciated as she is;
show the child that he is enjoyed as a contributing group member

By **being responsible**

Behaviour of child:
shows self discipline, accepts and works within limits,
uses initiative

Adult can:
encourage child to be involved in decision making process
help decide on limits and consequences
express confidence in the child

I BELONG

By **cooperating**

Behaviour of child:
plays and works effectively with others
able to share at appropriate times
is interested in cooperating

Adult can:
encourage all group members to work with one another
rather than compete against one another

By **being fair**

Behaviour of child:
returns kindness for hurt
ignores revengeful behaviour
withdraws from inappropriate conflict

Adult can:
encourage child's attitude by showing appreciation
provide a model of 'fairness'

Figure 6 Lifestyle perceptions — positive behaviour

Contribution

Children wanting attention, as all infants and children do, are able to gain it from being involved and *contributing* to the group or from *interactive and reciprocal play* with adults. When young children offer to help or are able to contribute to play, they are displaying a positive belief about themselves, that is: 'I can belong and get recognition from contributing'.

Responsive caregivers will encourage this positive behaviour by letting the children know they are appreciated and valued, and by giving them time. For instance, Marcus, 2½-years-old, tells the family day caregiver that he will 'help set the table'. Understanding and acknowledging his need for attention, the caregiver responds: 'Thank you Marcus. That will really help me to get lunch things ready for everyone today', thus encouraging and appreciating the *positive, contributive* behaviour from Marcus.

Responsibility

Likewise, young children whose purpose is to control and have power may be able to demonstrate this through acceptable responsible behaviours. Given the appropriate environment these children are able to show self-discipline, believing that they can be responsible for their own decisions and behaviour within the limits of the group. Responsive caregivers, aware of the purposes of behaviour, will recognise this goal in children and encourage them to be involved in making decisions. Thus the caregiver is expressing confidence in their ability to solve problems and become independent.

For example, Sally, aged 3-years, needs to feel she has some control and independence in her life. Fortunately, she has a responsive caregiver, James, who is aware of this, otherwise Sally and James may have found themselves constantly in power struggles. James has set limits, yet allows Sally to make her own choices within these limits whenever possible, so that Sally is developing responsibility and independence. For instance, James may ask: 'Where would you like to sit for lunch today Sally? . . . At Andrew's table or Jane's table?' or 'Sally, you need to put on a smock to do a fingerpainting. Would you like to choose the red smock or the blue smock?' Through incidental situations such as these, Sally is able to believe that she is recognised as having *acceptable control* over many aspects of her environment. With this encouragement Sally's behaviour will continue to be positive.

Cooperation

Joachim, a 4-year-old, is cooperating with other children and trying to resolve problem situations rather than retaliating. The responsive caregiver will be aware that Joachim's positive behaviour indicates his purpose is to belong or be socially accepted through being fair, rather than being revengeful.

Joachim's caregiver may notice that he attempts to share when playing with other children and will think of solutions to problems. For instance, Joachim and Patrick are building together in the block area. Joachim comments: 'Patrick, you could put your block there, and I'll add more here . . . then we'll make a garage that is bigger'. Later, Patrick hits out and argues that Joachim is using the black car that he wants. Joachim replies: 'What if I use the red one and you use the black one. We'll drive around the garage and then we can swap', instead of hitting back at Patrick.

The responsive caregiver will encourage Joachim's appropriate behaviour and let him know she appreciates his *cooperation and fairness*. For example, the caregiver may respond: 'Joachim, thank you for sharing with Patrick. Isn't it good when we can work together'.

Withdrawal from inappropriate conflict

Children who are able to withdraw at inappropriate times, such as during revengeful conflicts or physical aggression are demonstrating *their increasing maturity* with *positive behaviour*. These children have come to recognise the importance of 'standing back' from conflicts, while learning to verbally communicate their feelings in difficult situations.

For instance, Melissa, 6-years of age, is playing outside with three other children at family day care. Sandi wants Melissa to skip with her, but Melissa won't, so Sandi pushes her over. Melissa quietly responds: 'Sandy that hurts me when you push me. I don't feel like skipping right now but I might later'.

Responsive caregivers will themselves provide appropriate models for conflict resolution. By acknowledging feelings through reflective listening, caregivers will encourage *appropriate expression of feelings*, thus helping children and adults feel reassured and accepted.

Caregivers will encourage appropriate expression of feelings

CHAPTER 8:
Review activities

1 Describe what is meant by 'the basic motivation behind all behaviour is the desire to belong'.

2 Outline how a child's belief about belonging may influence her behaviour.

3 Identify the four categories of positive behaviour. Describe how a responsive caregiver will reinforce this behaviour.

Activities for further learning

1 Describe the positive goals and behaviours you are observing in children and adults around you.

2 Identify some techniques you could use to reinforce positive behaviour and write them down to remember for later use. You may wish to reflect on the ideas outlined in Section II: 'Developing Positive Relationships'.

3 Consider your own lifestyle beliefs and the goals of positive behaviour in yourself.

Recommended reading

Biddulph, S. *The Secret of Happy Children*, Chapter 2.
Dinkmeyer D. & McKay, G. *Systematic Training for Effective Parenting: Parent's Handbook*, Chapter 1.

9

*I*DENTIFYING GOALS OF MISBEHAVIOUR

After studying this chapter, the reader will be able to under-stand children's behaviour in the context of their need to be recognised and accepted within their social environment. Additionally, the reader will be able to describe the purposes of children's misbehaviour, identify the four broad goals of mis-behaviour, and learn of appropriate responses to these.

As described in Chapter 8, children are purposeful and goal-oriented individuals who need to feel accepted and to belong. The responses that children receive from people around them in the home, day care centre, family day care, kindergarten and school, will influence their beliefs about how they belong. Respon-sive caregivers will encourage children to gain recognition through positive behaviours.

Misbehaviour in children

Anti-social behaviour and misbehaviour are children's expression of their ways of seeking a place in the family or group, based on the mistaken belief that they cannot belong through constructive, cooperative or acceptable means.

Reflect again on the example given at the beginning of Chapter 8. Jodie, aged 2½-years, is left alone when she is playing quietly, yet when she whimpers and grizzles she is picked up and given attention. Jodie is beginning to use this behaviour constantly now so her quiet periods of play are less frequent. Being unsuccessful in her subconscious attempts to belong in positive ways, Jodie has become discouraged and has learned through trial and error that she will gain recognition from negative behaviour. According to Adlerian psychology, Jodie is developing a mistaken lifestyle belief that she belongs by behaving negatively.

Rudolf Dreikurs extended these Adlerian concepts and has presented a framework in which to understand negative behaviour by identifying four broad categories of typical misbehaviour. These categories represent what children want to happen based on their social motivation of belonging. Young children are not usually aware of the purposes of their behaviour, however they recognise that some actions bring reinforcement of belonging and acceptance, while others do not. Children quickly learn to repeat behaviour which appears to be successful or which works for them.

The four broad categories of typical misbehaviour identified are goals of *attention, power, revenge* and *assumed inadequacy*.

Not all negative behaviour is intentional misbehaviour. One must consider young children's developmental stages of understanding, ability to cope and skill acquisition. In Chapter 13: 'Age-appropriate planning', further descriptions of realistic expectations are included.

What is essential from infancy onwards, is that the significant people in children's lives respond to their behaviour in ways appropriate for encouraging positive behaviours, allowing children to feel accepted in this way. For example, 14-month-old Samuel may be a happy, contented child who demands little adult attention. One day he is frustrated by Shona, 18-months-old, sitting close to him and pulling his toys from him, so Samuel bites Shona. He not only gets a loud reaction from her, but the adults in the room also create a commotion about it. It may be that the next time Samuel wants attention he will again try this behaviour that caused such a reaction, even though he may have been punished for it. Thus, through repeated instances, young children's troublesome behaviour may become misbehaviour.

The essential aspect in all of this is the *reaction* from those around children. *If caregivers respond in a calm, low-key manner then children receive minimal or no reinforcement of their negative behaviour.*

So using the same example and the skills discussed in Chapters 5 and 7, Samuel could have been quietly moved to a different activity which would appropriately allow him to take out his frustrations.

The responsive and effective caregiver will be able to identify the purposes of children's behaviour from the feeling evoked by the behaviour, and will learn to respond in ways that will encourage children to gain recognition through acceptable means.

The four goals of misbehaviour

Attention

Three-year-old Ali needs to feel she belongs in the group at her early childhood centre. The sensitive caregiver responsible for Ali recognises this need in all the children. She deliberately and intentionally greets all children by name as they enter in the morning, and makes a positive comment about having them there. So the caregiver may say to Ali: 'Hello Ali, it's great to see you today . . . Your red ribbon is just the same colour as that fire engine puzzle over there . . . Would you like to go and have a look?' Later that morning while Ali is busy playing with two or three other children, the caregiver may go over to the group and say: 'Isn't it good when you can work together and make buildings like this . . . Ali, I like the way you've made . . .' Thus all children feel noticed and accepted. They know that they belong and gain attention through acceptable behaviours because of the caregiver's responsive attention.

However because of past reinforcement and perceptions, some children believe that in order to gain recognition or to be accepted they need to be the focus of attention or the one who is demanding service. Adult's responses to inappropriate attention-seeking behaviour usually reinforce the child's belief that this should be the pattern of her behaviour and the way to be part of the group. For example, Jeevika, aged 20-months, is sitting with two other children and a caregiver playing with manipulative activities. A typical almost-two-year-old, Jeevika enjoys being noticed and likes to have the caregiver's attention. She has made a small tower and says: 'Look, look', but the caregiver is talking with another child just then. Within seconds Jeevika has quietly but deliberately pinched the third child in the group. The caregiver speaks to Jeevika, and she continues with her play. A short time later Jeevika pokes the same child, and again is reprimanded.

A child displaying unacceptable behaviour to achieve the goal of attention has learnt that this usually gets her what she wants. She knows that if she keeps interrupting your story you will remind her, coax her, implore her to sit quietly, and she may for 30 seconds, but she has already had her misbehaviour reinforced through your coaxing. Instead, if she had either been ignored, or given an 'I' message or a choice about her continuing disruptive behaviour, she could then have experienced the consequences without gaining undue attention. These techniques will be described further in Chapters 10 and 11.

Behaviour which is directed towards achieving this goal usually *produces feelings of frustration and annoyance in adults* and thus we respond and reinforce inappropriately. We all need attention, and children need help to develop positive and appropriate ways of gaining attention by being encouraged and appreciated when cooperating and contributing acceptably.

Power

Children seek power as well as attention, as this gives them a sense of control over their environment. Consistent negative behaviour directed toward the goal of power occurs when previous inappropriate actions have been reinforced by others fighting with children about the behaviour, or giving in to children.

For instance, 2-year-old Robbie does not want to put her shoes on for going outside on a cold day. The caregiver knows that it is important for Robbie to have something on her feet when outside, so he may offer Robbie a choice: 'Robbie you can either put your shoes on and play outside, or you may stay inside and help Jenny put out the beds'. The caregiver may make a game of putting on Robbie's shoes, alternatively he may simply insist that she puts her shoes on and comes outside, causing Robbie to throw a tantrum. Or he may just give in, leaving Robbie to do as she wishes. In any case, Robbie is involving her caregiver in a power struggle and is learning that power is her way of belonging here.

Children whose behaviour fits into this category are those who wish to control and be the boss, which may be fine if this goal is achieved through acceptable means. However, the child who behaves unacceptably is learning to have her goal reinforced in this way. This child believes that because certain behaviours have worked in the past for her, the way for her to belong to the group is by being the boss. She may throw a tantrum to show she is boss or she may simply refuse to cooperate. In either situation she is likely to cause the *caregiver to feel angry and want to be involved in a power struggle*. It is important to avoid becoming involved as it serves to reinforce the child's belief that this is how to gain recognition and acceptance.

The 'power' child needs to be given opportunities for decision making from responsible choices at appropriate times. When behaviour is inappropriate, withdraw from the contest. Later use guidance methods to reinforce acceptable behaviour such as offering choices, allowing the child to experience consequences, acknowledging the child's feelings, redirecting or 'I' messages.

Revenge

Misbehaviour which has revenge as its purpose is a more complex emotional goal not normally seen in infants, but it may begin evolving during early childhood. This is usually displayed by children who are feeling discouraged and angry at someone or something. This child behaves in a way which shows she wants to hurt others the way she feels hurt or to retaliate at someone, even though her behaviour may be directed at someone or something different.

For instance, 5-year-old Kathy has become discouraged and is displaying a considerable amount of negative behaviour. Her parents are angry and frustrated, and are continually getting cross. Through past reinforcement Kathy believes that she gains recognition when getting back, or hurting, other people. When Kathy's Dad takes her to the day care centre, and Dan, the caregiver, greets her at the door, Kathy turns around, kicks Dan and says: 'I hate you Dan', stamping over to another caregiver *and making Dan feel distressed and guilty.* Her purpose is to hurt and in the past she has gained distressed or guilty responses to her behaviour, which of course reinforces her goal. In order to help her change her behaviour caregivers need to avoid being hurt or feeling guilty, thus not reinforcing her belief that she is belonging to the group or being noticed by showing revenge.

The 'revenge' child needs to be given lots of opportunities where she can feel good about herself and where she is encouraged. Her feelings need to be acknowledged as was described in Chapter 7, and inappropriate behaviour redirected without it being given undue attention.

When children like this are in their care, caregivers need support and encouragement from their peers in order to not feel hurt and discouraged.

Assumed inadequacy

As with children displaying the goal of revenge, these young children are usually feeling very discouraged with a low self-esteem. This goal of assumed inadequacy is not normally seen in infants. Because of past reinforcement, they believe they belong through gaining attention and recognition by being unable and incapable. In other words, they have discovered that by withdrawing from responsibilities or participation, they can in fact avoid effort, yet still gain attention because *people will pity them and thus do things for them.*

For example, Mario, aged 5-years, is asked to put on his tracksuit ready to go outside. Mario simply stands beside his bed looking at his tracksuit. He may attempt to put his legs into the pants, but if his goal is assumed inadequacy you can be sure he won't succeed.

The pitying adult may come over feeling disappointed that Mario 'can't' put his clothes on, and will quickly do it for him. However, the responsive caregiver will be aware that Mario is able to dress himself given time and encouragement. She puts Mario's track-suit out and calmly says that children who are dressed will be able to go outside for afternoon tea. She does not expect perfect-ion in his dressing and encourages his efforts.

It is wrong of adults to reinforce this mistaken belief by accept-ing a child's consistent inability or withdrawal. When a child is displaying this goal, the adult *tends to feel as if the child really is hope-less, helpless and unable.* Instead, adults need to offer encouragement, avoid doing things for the child that she could do herself, for example, feeding and dressing, and ensure that they are provid-ing experiences and challenges appropriate to that child's level. This child needs help to start feeling good about herself again.

If caregivers *genuinely* believe that a child is unable, then assumed inadequacy is unlikely to be the child's purpose. Children need to have times which are set aside as informal teaching and learn-ing opportunities, in order to develop skills and appropriate behaviours.

For instance, in the above situation, if Mario at 5-years of age is genuinely unable to dress himself in simple clothes, then he needs assistance in developing these skills. However the time to teach is not when he is being noticed through being incapable, as this will simply reinforce his belief that he is inadequate. The responsive caregiver will plan part of her future program around Mario's needs, including other children as appropriate.

Misbehaviour as a lifestyle perception

Although they are usually unaware of their goals, children will continue to repeat behaviours which are reinforced, whether it be positive or negative reinforcement. Thus, if they believe that they only receive attention or 'belong' to the group when behav-

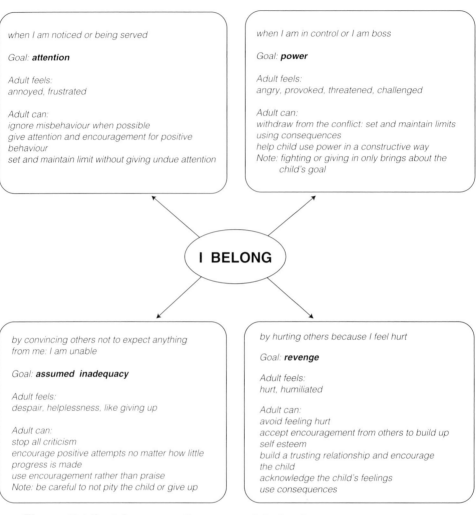

when I am noticed or being served

Goal: **attention**

Adult feels:
annoyed, frustrated

Adult can:
ignore misbehaviour when possible
give attention and encouragement for positive
behaviour
set and maintain limit without giving undue attention

when I am in control or I am boss

Goal: **power**

Adult feels:
angry, provoked, threatened, challenged

Adult can:
withdraw from the conflict: set and maintain limits
using consequences
help child use power in a constructive way
Note: fighting or giving in only brings about the
child's goal

I BELONG

*by convincing others not to expect anything
from me: I am unable*

Goal: **assumed inadequacy**

Adult feels:
despair, helplessness, like giving up

Adult can:
stop all criticism
encourage positive attempts no matter how little
progress is made
use encouragement rather than praise
Note: be careful to not pity the child or give up

by hurting others because I feel hurt

Goal: **revenge**

Adult feels:
hurt, humiliated

Adult can:
avoid feeling hurt
accept encouragement from others to build up
self esteem
build a trusting relationship and encourage
the child
acknowledge the child's feelings
use consequences

Figure 7 Lifestyle perceptions — misbehaviour

ing in this manner, then these inappropriate behaviours will be continued. This is a consequence of children's faulty beliefs about themselves, developed from their own perceptions of their lifestyle. Although we do not cause children to misbehave, we reinforce and encourage their misbehaviour and faulty beliefs by reacting in an expected manner.

Figure 7 represents children's mistaken lifestyle perceptions about their way of belonging in a particular social situation; for example 'I belong when I am being noticed'.

In order to respond appropriately to children's goals of misbehaviour, it is necessary to initially examine your *own feelings* about the child's behaviour, then *identify the child's goal* and *respond* accordingly. To change a child's behaviour, it is necessary to first change our own way of responding.

CHAPTER 9:
Review activities

1 Describe what is meant by a 'mistaken lifestyle belief'.

2 What is 'misbehaviour'? Consider whether all inappropriate behaviour is misbehaviour.

3 Identify the four broad categories of typical misbehaviour, and describe an adult's feelings about the behaviours.

4 How can a responsive and effective caregiver reinforce positive behaviour rather than misbehaviour?

Activities for further learning

1 Using the caregiver's feelings as a guide, *identify the goals of behaviour* in the following situations:
(a) Ken, the caregiver, has set up the water play inside and children wanting to participate will need to wear a waterproof smock. Mandy, 3-years of age, refuses to put on a smock but simply looks at Ken and begins playing. When Ken again asks her to put on a smock, Mandy turns around and defiantly says: 'No!', making Ken feel really mad.
(b) Matt, 3-years-old, consistently leaves his lunch sitting in front of him. When Sally, the caregiver, gives him a spoon he disinterestedly picks it up waiting for her to feed him instead. Sally feels sorry for Matt because he doesn't appear to be able to do things for himself.

(c) Tina, 5-years-old, has a new baby, Mark, at home and there have been lots of relatives visiting and fussing over Mark. When she is playing with other children Tina may suddenly turn and bite or scratch, she has even started breaking their toys. Tina's Mum feels really distressed as she wants Tina to play appropriately with others.

(d) A caregiver is telling a story to a small group of four-year-old children, when one of them, Jason, starts calling out and interrupting. When asked to stop, he does for about 15 seconds but then keeps doing it. The caregiver is beginning to feel annoyed and frustrated by Jason's constant interruptions.

2 Apply your own understanding of goals of misbehaviour to your own situations:

(a) Describe a young child's behaviour which is a problem.

(b) Consider your feelings when the child behaves in this way.

(c) Identify the child's likely mistaken belief about belonging, reflecting on the purposes of misbehaviour.

(d) Consider an alternative response which would be appropriate. Next time the child misbehaves in this way use your alternative approach.

3 Use the above steps to identify a child's belief about belonging through positive behaviour, then consider how you would reinforce those positive behaviours.

Recommended reading

Balson, M. *Becoming Better Parents*, Chapters 3 and 4.
Biddulph, S. *The Secret of Happy Children*, Chapter 2.
Dinkmeyer, D. & McKay, G. *Systematic Training for Effective Parenting: Parent's Handbook*. Chapter 1.

■ *SECTION III* ■

UNDERSTANDING CHILDREN'S BEHAVIOUR

Summary

Young children are usually unaware of the purposes of their behaviour. Babies are unlikely to be intentionally misbehaving but are beginning to discover which behaviours do or do not work. However all children soon become aware of the reactions they get from caregivers around them.

Children who are encouraged and who feel accepted and valued are more likely to behave appropriately. Positive behaviour can be broadly categorised according to the following goals: contribution, responsibility, cooperation and withdrawal from inappropriate conflict. Responsive and effective caregivers will respond positively to children demonstrating these goals, appreciating and encouraging their behaviour.

Misbehaviour can be broadly categorised under one of the following goals: attention, power, revenge and assumed inadequacy. Children are usually unaware of their goals but continue to repeat misbehaviour because of reinforcement. Caregivers may be able to identify the goal by their feelings about it, then change children's misbehaviour by learning to respond to these goals in different ways. They will be able to reinforce appropriate behaviour through positive and encouraging responses.

■ *S E C T I O N   IV* ■

RESPONDING WITH
GUIDANCE TECHNIQUES

Focus

If young children grow up believing in themselves, their skills and their ability to contribute in a socially acceptable manner, then society as a whole will benefit from these competent individuals. Adults, who are aware of and put into practice skills of positive guidance, will be able to provide a secure, nurturing environment which allows for this optimum social development.

Chapter 10 focuses on the development of self-discipline and independence through effective communication and realistic limits. Chapter 11 clarifies the concept of behavioural consequences as a positive guidance technique to be used instead of punishment. Chapter 12 examines the relevant factors that influence conflict resolution and describes the method of exploring alternatives to assist children to resolve problems themselves. Using these methods, responsive and effective caregivers will assist the development, responsibility and mutual respect in children.

$$\boxed{10}$$

USING LIMIT-SETTING TECHNIQUES

After studying this chapter, the reader will be able to understand the importance of positive guidance for infants and young children through identifying skills of encouragement, redirection and effective communication.

The goal of effective guidance is to assist children in becoming confident, fully-functioning individuals who can make decisions and direct themselves appropriately. Young children are enormously influenced by their social environment, giving those who interact with children a responsibility to create an appropriate atmosphere using sensitive and effective guidance skills.

Effective guidance

Guidance encompasses all the adult does or says to influence children's behaviour, either directly or indirectly. It is more positive and constructive than 'discipline', which usually carries connotations of punishment and restriction. Discipline limits the development of responsibility and decision making.

Effective guidance is based on previously identified skills and values considered to purposely promote appropriate behaviour. Responsive caregivers will consider their own behaviour initially, and then explore personal changes they may make to encourage positive behaviour in children. As was discussed in Section III, not all inappropriate behaviour is misbehaviour and caregivers need to reflect on their knowledge, understanding and expectations of young children before determining appropriate limits.

Responsive and effective guidance will be neither autocratic nor chaotic; rather it will be based on the domestic values of social equality, trust, cooperation, shared responsibility and freedom to make choices within acceptable limits, as outlined in Section I. There is no place or need for corporal punishment, physical or verbal abuse, sarcasm or emotional deprivation in an effectively functioning home or early childhood centre.

A supportive, secure environment is established through the development and maintenance of relationships as described in Section II, by developing an understanding of children's behaviour as identified in Section III, and by using sensitive guidance skills with realistic limits.

Limits are designed to protect the safety of children and adults, and to assist young children to grow toward self-control and self-discipline. Appropriate limits are essential to the functioning of a cooperative society providing order without chaos. For instance, if I decide I will drive my car on the wrong side of the road because I feel like doing it, what is likely to happen? I am likely to jeopardise my own and other people's safety. In all aspects of life, in order to live cooperatively with others there must be agreed rules to which we adhere. Limits are similar to a set of rules that are flexible enough to be extended and adapted as children grow and mature (as was shown in Figure 1).

Limits applying to infants

Infants and very young children need clear and definite limits, requiring very simple explanations, that will allow them to develop trust in adults and security in their environment. For example Toby,

9-months-old and mobile, wants to explore his environment. However there are dangers from which he needs to be protected. Toby's caregiver, Tania, has provided a simple and safe room for the infants but Toby wants to investigate the power switch. Tania quickly and distinctly says 'Toby' to initially distract him while she is walking over. As she picks him up and moves him away, Tania gently yet firmly comments: 'Toby, that power switch is dangerous . . . I can't let you play there. Come and I'll put you beside this playboard with knobs and switches'.

In this way Tania has provided a definite limit while allowing Toby to continue exploring in a different way.

Limits applying to toddlers

Toddlers desiring independence and autonomy require limits which offer safe investigation of both the environment and the people within it, while allowing them choices in decision making. Limits for toddlers will be firm on the outside, yet flexible on the inside. That is, toddlers will have opportunities to test the limits but there will be a point beyond which there is no choice. For instance, Nyssa, 2½-years-old, wants to go outside on a cold day in his underclothes. Nyssa's caregiver, knowing that toddlers like to feel in control, puts out two different sets of clothes for Nyssa to choose from and then enthusiastically says: 'Nyssa, it's going to be such fun outside today. Would you like to help me move the slide?'

Nyssa quickly chooses his clothes and begins to dress himself. The caregiver could not allow Nyssa to go beyond the limit of not wearing clothes outside on a cold day, although if appropriate she may have allowed Nyssa to simply remain inside. However, she did allow Nyssa to make decisions and assert his independence within acceptable boundaries.

Limits applying to preschoolers

Preschool-age children are developing more mature intellectual skills, allowing them to contribute meaningfully to decision-making.

They are able to think through situations, often using the boundaries imposed by appropriate limits as part of their imaginative games and play. For example, 5-year-old Anya may be playing with a group of peers outside. Anya is aware that the wheel toys need to stay on the paths so that other children are safe. This is one of the limits that had been decided upon by all children in the group at her centre. Anya and her friends use initiative and imagination in incorporating the paths into their motorcycle game. The responsive caregiver will be aware of this imaginative play and encourages their responsible self-disciplined behaviour through enthusiastic comments like: 'I like where your motorcycles are going . . . What if we get some chalk and draw lines on the paths? Where would you like them? Could we put some traffic lights in?' And so on.

Effective limits

Effective limits will encompass the following values based on respect and equality. *Children may neither deliberately do things which will hurt themselves or someone else, nor may they intentionally cause damage or hurt to animals, materials or equipment.* On the other hand, limits that are mostly for the convenience of caregivers should be reconsidered with the children's needs foremost.

Clear verbal and physical direction of what is acceptable is essential when conveying effective limits to infants and children. Infants are egocentric and so lack understanding of others around them, thus needing caregivers who will ensure these limits are followed through. For instance, Connie and Leigh, both 12-months-old, are playing with wooden pegs on the floor, when Connie uses the pegs to hit Leigh. Jackie, the caregiver, immediately moves to these children and quietly speaks to Connie: 'Connie, it seems like you feel like banging the pegs onto something . . . here's a saucepan for you', while showing Connie how she can bang the pegs onto a saucepan to make a noise, Jackie has successfully distracted Connie from hurting Leigh and redirected her attention to another activity, thus enforcing a limit in a positive, acceptable way.

Redirection

Greta, aged about 3, is having a difficult morning. She has been hitting some other children and just now she has gone over to the block corner and knocked over Tom's blocks. The caregiver comes up to Greta and says, 'Greta, it looks like you are feeling really mad. It seems like you want to hit out at things. Let's go and set up the punching bag and you can hit at that as much as you'd like to. I can't let you hit Tom, and it upsets him when you knock his building down. Let's get the punching bag.'

This is an example of redirection. Redirection of unacceptable behaviour is an effective method of positive guidance in responsive caregiving. It means attempting to turn the child's attention from unacceptable behaviour to an experience or behaviour that is acceptable. This alternative experience should be equally as interesting to the child, thus allowing an outlet for the child's feelings. Unfortunately there have been situations when behaviour such as the above example has happened and the caregiver has inappropriately said to the child, 'Come on Greta, you need to come over here. Sit down and read a book.' How would you respond if you were feeling mad and aggressive and someone said, 'Come and sit quietly and read a book'? This is not effective redirection — it is simply negating the child's strong feelings and occupying her quietly, whereas redirection promotes prosocial behaviour in children.

Adults need to interpret the child's behaviour, being receptive to her underlying need, either emotional or physical — and express this through a reflective statement which effectively acknowledges the child's feelings. For redirecting to be effective, it must be logically related to the child's behaviour. For example, the child who is hitting is obviously feeling angry or frustrated, so an outlet for those feelings would be to redirect attention to the clay, or punching bag, or hammering and so on.

What is redirection?

Redirection is about channelling children's feeling into appropriate ways of behaving. When you are interacting with preschoolers and older children, you can then talk about other ways of managing their behaviour, but in the first instance you want to give them an outlet for this inappropriate behaviour.

Redirection is a very useful strategy with infants, particularly when caregivers are able to acknowledge children's feelings and then redirect them to an activity with a similar outlet for their feelings.

How is redirection implemented?

Using the earlier example of Greta and Tom we can consider the sequence for effective redirection.

* *Identify the child's need/feeling*

'Greta, age about 3 years, is having a difficult morning. She has been hitting some other children and just now she has gone over to the block corner and knocked over Tom's blocks.' The caregiver was aware of Greta's needs and perceptively responded to them. In this situation Greta needed an outlet for her needs rather than being encouraged to verbalise her feelings, as might be done under other circumstances.

* *Acknowledge that feeling*

'Greta, it looks like you are feeling really mad.' The caregiver gave a simple statement acknowledging Greta's feelings.

* *Consider an alternative acceptable outlet for channelling the child's feelings*

'It seems like you want to hit out at things. Let's go and set up the punching bag . . .'

The caregiver suggested an alternative outlet for Greta's feelings. The caregiver could also have asked Greta herself to suggest an alternative behaviour, as is described in a later chapter on conflict resolution.

* *State the alternative action or behaviour in a calm and positive manner*

'Let's go and set up the punching bag and you can hit that as much as you'd like to.'

The caregiver is calmly stating the acceptable outlet.

* *With very young children the adult respectfully moves the child to, or gives the child, the acceptable alternative*

If Greta had been an infant or younger child, the caregiver might have simultaneously moved her away to an acceptable alternative whilst calmly talking with her.

- *With older children, only give a choice of actions if you really mean the child to choose for herself*

As suggested in the third step, the caregiver could have explored alternatives with Greta, enabling Greta to select an appropriate outlet herself. This is particularly useful with older children.

- *Be calm and reassuring, helping the child feel confident and comfortable*

'I can't let you hit Tom, and it upsets him when you knock his building down.'

The caregiver responded in a calm manner enabling Greta to retain her dignity and confidence.

- *Periodically check the child's involvement, offering encouragement for self-control, self-direction and responsibility*

'Let's get the punching bag.' This respectful response promotes acceptance and could be followed on with the caregiver's acknowledgement of Greta's use of the punching bag.

Redirection is a very useful strategy with infants, particularly if caregivers are able to acknowledge children's feelings, then redirect them to an activity with a similar outlet for their feelings, such as Connie banging the pegs on a saucepan instead of on to Leigh.

Distraction

Redirection is not distraction. When we distract a child, we are simply changing the focus of the child's attention. For example, George who is going around pulling people's hair can be distracted by saying, 'George, did you see that red fire engine go past?' It takes George's mind off what he is doing and it may well stop him from continuing the anti-social activity of hair pulling. But is it really helping George to cope with his feelings? Is it giving him an outlet for his frustration?

George could have been redirected to an activity which allowed him to take out some aggression in an acceptable manner, such as pounding the clay, splashing soapy water or pulling and pushing on pieces of rope.

However, distraction can be a useful guidance technique particularly with infants. For example, 10-month-old Alysha is finding it difficult to separate from her mother. Even though Mum stays around for a while in the mornings, as soon as she says goodbye Alysha cries uncontrollably for a few minutes. Vince, the caregiver, holds Alysha very warmly and securely, acknowledging her feelings of distress, whilst at the same time attempting to distract her attention to another focus. He calmly and respectfully says, 'Alysha, it looks like you're feeling so miserable because Mummy has gone to work. Let's go and see what the big children are doing out in the playground.'

Whatever the technique used, young children require clear, positive guidelines as to what is acceptable behaviour, as was described in Chapter 7. Before commencing an activity with children discuss what is acceptable with them, so introducing the limits for that particular activity.

For example, Franca, the caregiver, may be wishing to tell a story to a small group of preschool aged children and believes they can be involved in decision making about appropriate behaviour. Franca may introduce the idea when sitting at the children's level with them: 'I'd like to tell you a story with puppets. It's about five children who go for a picnic . . . I really want everyone to be able to hear this story so what do you think you'll have to do? (be quiet) . . . Do you think other children will be able to see my hands moving if some of you wriggle around? (no) . . . So how will we sit? (still) . . . So it seems like we're going to have a lovely story if everyone can sit quietly and still. Does that sound okay?'

Older preschool children will be able to discuss not only the appropriate limits, but also the consequences of children *not* responding to limits. So in the previous example Franca may then say: 'What do you think we should do if people keep interrupting our story?'

The responsive caregiver will be aware that children want to belong to the group and be a part of it, with peer group influence being very powerful. Through effective leadership and clear communication, caregivers are able to have preschool children making choices about limits, consequences and appropriate behaviours within defined boundaries. The idea of behavioural consequences as a positive guidance technique is discussed in Chapter 11: 'Using behavioural consequences'.

Caregivers will let children know they are appreciated through verbal and non-verbal behaviour

Caregivers will *reinforce* appropriate behaviours by using 'I' messages and encouragement techniques as previously described. They will let children know they are appreciated, encouraging cooperative behaviour and adherence to reasonable limits. For instance, when children are playing imaginatively, yet appropriately, in the digging patch, the caregiver may quietly comment: 'I'm really pleased to see that you're able to keep the spades down lower than your shoulders. It means that you are digging safely here . . . thank you'.

Through respect, encouragement and cooperation, children will develop appropriate behaviour. This will be maintained within a sensitively structured environment, as is described in Chapter 13. Responsive guidance is based on positive communication skills and realistic expectations of young children.

CHAPTER 10:
Review activities

1 Describe the goal of effective guidance of infants and young children.

2 Identify at least two reasons why limits are necessary.

3 Name three guidance strategies that you would consider appropriate to use with preschool children.

4 Outline how limits vary for different ages/stages of children.

5 Describe what is meant by 'redirection'.

6 How can encouragement be used as a guidance technique?

Activities for further learning

1 Observe a group of young children and consider how the strategies discussed in this chapter would be appropriately applied to their behaviour.

2 Plan a group experience for two to six children. Identify and write down your expected limits before beginning the experience. Decide how you will communicate the limits to the children and how you may offer choices.

3 Identify situations in your own caregiving where you could reinforce limits by using encouragement and showing appreciation.

Recommended reading

Dinkmeyer, D. & McKay, G. *Systematic Training for Effective Parenting: Parent's Handbook*, Chapter 5.

CHAPTER

$$\boxed{11}$$

USING BEHAVIOURAL CONSEQUENCES

After studying this chapter, the reader will be able to understand the concept of behavioural consequences as a positive guidance technique. By this means children learn to be responsible and make appropriate decisions themselves, without the need for punishment.

The need for a democratic environment

Young children are striving to find their identity and assert their independence. They need to be given opportunities for this within a safe, democratic environment, which allows them to select some behaviours or actions over others, to make decisions, and to experience the outcomes of their choices.

In traditional, autocratic settings adults make decisions for children based upon a superior adult–inferior child relationship. Thus young children are not provided with opportunities to develop skills of self-discipline, responsibility or independence. The traditional and autocratic method of discipline is for the caregiver to reward children when they obey and to punish when they disobey.

For instance, Davita is responsible for a group of preschool children playing in the sandpit. Lucinda and Pierre begin throwing sand at one another, so Davita quickly intervenes, angrily saying: 'Lucinda and Pierre, go inside this minute. You know you shouldn't throw sand'. Later, when it is afternoon tea time, Davita hands out icy poles to the children who were 'playing nicely' in the sandpit, while Pierre and Lucinda look on.

There are several significant reasons for not using this method in a democratic and mutually respectful environment.

Most punishment, such as the instance described, is decided on by the adult determining an outcome not related to the inappropriate behaviour. This gives credence to the belief that being an adult means to be superior and do as you wish, rather than believing that adults take on effective and responsible leadership roles. It limits children in their capacity for decision making because the adult does all the deciding, using punishment as a means of suppressing unacceptable behaviour. Responsive caregivers will be encouraging children to accept age-appropriate responsibility for their own behaviour.

Children used to punishment and reward soon discover that they only need to obey when the adult is around in order to be rewarded. Responsive caregivers will reinforce children's appropriate behaviour as an accepted part of creating a cooperative situation, where children, guided by others, develop self-discipline.

Behavioural consequences

Behavioural consequences are ways of stimulating actions in children as they make decisions about particular behaviours. The basis of this approach is that all behaviour is shaped and maintained by its associated consequences. In a democratic situation where there is freedom with order, children have the right to make choices about their behaviour. Thus, reflecting on the previous example of Lucinda and Pierre in the sandpit, observing their inappropriate behaviour Davita may say: 'Lucinda and Pierre, when you throw sand I feel concerned because it may get in someone's eyes . . . You can either use the sand for digging and making things, or you can leave the sandpit and go and use the ball for throwing'.

It is then up to Pierre and Lucinda which they decide to do, both actions are acceptable, but there is no other choice. If they decide to remain in the sandpit, Davita will *encourage* their appropriate behaviour. However if they continue to throw sand she will respond while moving them away: 'It seems like you have decided not to stay in the sandpit . . . so you can go to the storeroom and get the ball for throwing. You're welcome to come back to the sandpit later'.

Thus Lucinda and Pierre learn from the consequential results of their choice of behaviours, and it is their responsibility to change it if they wish.

This method differs from reward and punishment because it holds children responsible for their own behaviour, while allowing them to make decisions about appropriate actions.

Children are able to accept responsibility for their own behaviour and feel good about themselves when you offer them choices within acceptable limits. Let children make and accept decisions by giving them appropriate choices, and then allow them to accept the consequences of their decision. If the child is not happy with the consequences of a decision, make it clear that she is welcome to choose differently next time.

For instance, a caregiver may say: 'Katie, you may either come inside for a story or stay outside and play'. A choice is offered, but once others are inside and having a story, Katie needs to accept the consequences and should not come and interrupt. Therefore, the caregiver will say: 'I'm sorry Katie, but you will have to wait until we have another story later'. She will help the child accept the consequences of her choice and to understand that a different decision can be made next time.

Through caregivers using behavioural consequences as a guidance technique, children are able to choose to behave in a particular way. They know that they will be expected to experience the consequences of that choice and that this consequence is related to the behaviour.

Choices and consequences encourage children to be responsible by offering freedom within limits. With young children over

Responsive caregivers will encourage children to accept age-appropriate responsibility for their own behaviour

about 2-years of age, responsibility for much behaviour can be given to the child rather than the adult, thus encouraging independence, autonomy and a feeling of control over their environments.

As has been described in other chapters, infants have yet to reach a level of intellectual and logical reasoning where understanding of limits occurs. Although there is always an outcome as a consequence of an infant's behaviour, it cannot be assumed that the infant understands the relationship. For example, 6-month-old Edwinda pulls the cat's tail and the cat scratches her. Edwina notices and is hurt by the outcome of her behaviour. However at this age she may not connect her action with that of the cat, unless she repeats it again and again.

This inability to relate consequences to behaviour should not preclude caregivers from acting on infant behaviour. Given warm and sensitive relationships and positive non-verbal communication, infants will learn of the results of their behaviour through

Through using behavioural consequences children will learn about responsible behaviour and make appropriate decisions

caregivers accepting responsibility on their behalf. In the previous example, the responsive caregiver will act on Edwina's behaviour by gently, yet firmly, saying: 'That hurts the cat, Edwina' while at the same time moving either Edwina or the cat.

There are two types of behavioural consequence through which children learn about responsible and appropriate decisions.

Natural consequences

These occur as a result of the child's behaviour without the intervention of another person. For example, the child who refuses to put rain gear on to go outside gets wet, or the child who refuses to eat goes hungry until the next meal. The adult does not need to become involved. There is one exception to using natural consequences as a learning experience, and that is in situations of danger, safety or emergency. Then intervention or logical consequences should be substituted immediately.

Logical consequences

These require the intervention of another person, usually the caregiver, and focus on the reality in the social situation of freedom with order.

Applying logical consequences acknowledges mutual rights, mutual respect and responsibility. To be effective, children must be able to see them as being logically related to their inappropriate behaviour. That is, the consequence must fit the behaviour.

A logical consequence of a child using blocks to hit another child instead of building with them, would be for the child to choose to either play with blocks properly or leave the block area. The child should go somewhere else, preferably where she can take out her aggression, such as pounding clay, hammering or punching a punch bag.

A caregiver, having observed the incident, may say: 'Milly, when you hit Sam with the blocks I feel worried because he might get hurt . . . You can either use the blocks for building or you can go and hammer . . . It is up to you'.

Logical consequences can become punishments if the caregiver threatens or is hostile, or if no choice is given. The objective is to encourage children to make responsible decisions, not to force or scare them into submission.

However, once choices have been given, the caregiver does not need to keep repeating them, otherwise children soon become 'caregiver deaf'. Caregivers will find themselves saying: 'Milly, remember what I said . . . Milly, I said you can either . . .' and so on. Of course Milly remembers what was said, but she is now involved in a successful power struggle where she controls the situation.

There is a definite method to successfully applying logical consequences incorporating the following sequence:

□ Use an 'I' *message*, as described in Chapter 7, to let children know how you feel about their inappropriate behaviour. For instance, Brian, 4-years-old, is picking up pieces of a puzzle and throwing them from the table onto the floor. So the caregiver calmly says: 'When you throw the puzzles onto the floor I feel concerned that they will get lost'.

□ Provide *acceptable choices* in a respectful and calm manner. 'You can either use the pieces to fit the puzzles together or we can put the puzzles into the storeroom for now.'

□ Allow the child to *choose* then follow through with the *consequence,* giving the child the assurance that they will have the opportunity to change the decision later, but not immediately. So if Brian continues to throw the pieces, the caregiver will say: 'It seems like you've decided that the puzzles should be put away, perhaps we can get them out again after morning tea'.

□ Then if the misbehaviour is repeated, follow through again but extend the time that will elapse before the child can try again, depending on the age of the child. 'It seems like you're still not ready to use these puzzles properly. We can get them out again tomorrow'.

The responsive caregiver will also acknowledge Brian's feelings while redirecting his behaviour into an appropriate outlet. So it might be suggested that he goes to the water play where he can drop things into the water to see their effect. For instance: 'Hey, look Brian, you could come over here and plonk things into the water. I wonder what will float and what will sink'.

Applying behavioural consequences offers an effective guidance technique which encourages a positive self-concept in both children and caregivers. It is impersonal and there is no guilt attached. Children are able to retain their self-esteem by not being labelled or classified for their inappropraite actions, and caregivers have no need to feel like ogres or nags.

Consequences or time-out?

'Time-out' is a phrase often used by people believing that, in certain instances, some children just need time and space to be alone. However, young children may misinterpret this time-out notion as a sign of public rejection or humiliation.

When children's misbehaviour is affecting or interfering with others, then they are demonstrating neither respect nor cooperation. To simply remove them or send them away may only intensify negative behaviour at other times. These misbehaving children are likely to be discouraged and lacking in self-esteem. As was shown in Chapters 6 and 8, if young children are to be assisted in developing alternative behaviour patterns, then encouragement of a positive self-image is necessary.

If children's negative behaviour is clearly interfering with other children's rights, then caregivers do need to act. However when caring for a group of children it is *inappropriate* to put a child in a room alone as a punishment (for example an office, bathroom or corridor). This may cause unnecessary emotional suffering and rejection. The responsive caregiver will consider goals of behaviour and what the child's negative behaviour actually demonstrates. Does she need some space just to herself to play independently? Does the child need time alone, listening to music or looking at books? Perhaps she is really tired and just needs to be quietly and calmly tucked into bed? Maybe she could quietly withdraw to another area with a caregiver.

As an example consider Helen, 2½-years-old, who has been biting and disrupting the play of other children. The caregivers have attempted to redirect Helen and to reassure the other children, but understandably they now feel they just want to put Helen into the bathroom and tell her to stay there until she can behave. This solution may leave the room calm for a short time, but it may also leave Helen feeling confused, rejected and possibly even more determined to 'get back'. Consider what Helen's goal may be then!

An alternative approach is to ensure that Helen feels welcome and noticed amongst the group of children. Help her to feel good about herself and provide her with activities which will allow her to take out aggression acceptably. If Helen continues to act disruptively so that other children are affected, the caregiver will quietly move down to Helen and acknowledge her feelings: 'Helen, it seems like you're feeling really mad this morning and you're hurting people around you. I can't let you hurt Jacob and Rocco. Let's find you something to do where you don't need to be near anyone else'. This may be a bowl of warm soapy water or a sand tray placed at the side of the room just for 'one child only — space alone play'. The caregiver will take Helen to the activity, letting her know she can play there and when she is ready to play without hurting other children, she is welcome to come back. The caregiver is thus assisting Helen to be responsible for her own behaviour and develop self-discipline. The caregiver may quietly say: 'When you are ready to play with Jacob and Rocco without hurting them, you can come and tell me, then we'll go back over there'.

With careful pre-planning responsive caregivers will be able to set up 'one child only — space alone' activity areas in their playrooms and so withdraw the disruptive child without removing her completely, thus giving time-out an alternative focus.

CHAPTER 11:
Review activities

1 Describe what is meant by 'behavioural consequences' and why this technique is appropriate to democratic caregiving.

2 Outline three significant differences between punishment and consequences.

3 Identify the two types of consequences, then describe how each helps children learn responsibility and self-discipline.

4 Outline the sequence typically used when applying logical consequences.

Activities for further learning

1 Consider the following situations and decide on an appropriate consequence for each. Practice how you would express it in order to effectively guide children's behaviour by giving them a clear choice of behaviours.
  (a) John, aged 3 years, is playing at the water trough. You have talked about limits with the children, and asked John several times to be careful because he is wetting other children. How would you apply consequences?
  (b) Sophie, aged 4 years, is flicking the finger paint over other children waking past and the furniture. How would you apply consequences?
  (c) Jane, aged 2 years, refuses to eat the food that has been prepared for lunch. How would you apply consequences?

2 Imagine you are planning a group experience for five 4-year-old children. Identify and write down *your* expected limits before beginning the experience. Decide:
  (a) how you will communicate the limits to the children
  (b) how you might guide inappropriate behaviour by using the sequence outlined in applying logical consequences.

Recommended reading

Balson, M. *Becoming Better Parents*, Chapter 6.
Dinkmeyer D. & McKay, G. *Systematic Training for Effective Parenting: Parent's Handbook*, Chapter 6.

CHAPTER

12

THE CONFLICT DILEMMA

A group of 3-year-olds are playing outside and some of them are on the bikes. Two of these children are fighting over the only 'big' bike in the playground. Maria, the physically bigger child is trying to pull the bike away from Rachel. Rachel hits back screaming, 'No, I want it! I want it! It's mine!' The caregiver walks over and says, 'Maria, Rachel had the bike first. Give it back. You can have a turn later.' Maria refuses and a struggle results. The caregiver again says, 'Maria, it's Rachel's turn. You can go and sit inside and wait.' Maria walks away with her head down, destroying a child's block construction on her way through. How can the responsive adult assist children in resolving disputes such as this?

Conflict resolution in a democratic early childhood service

Prosocial behaviour does not just happen by putting children in situations, then setting the limits. The adult has the responsibility to actually make it happen. Children are being given all sorts of different messages from our society and from their environments. They see people on television achieving what they want by power, by superiority, by force. They see adults getting their own way, by using their stronger and more superior skill. This creates a dilemma for some children as to what is appropriate in sorting out problems. Some discouraged children find their only sense of belonging is by being difficult and their only source of power is to refuse to cooperate. These children are in particular need of assistance towards prosocial behaviour through our encouragement and nurturing guidance, not through adult power or superiority.

Prosocial behaviour is that which is socially acceptable within a given situation. Although most children have a natural inclination towards compassion and acceptance of others, strategies for favourable behaviour need to be promoted by adults. Children need to achieve a feeling of 'win–win' through resolving disputes acceptably, emerging from a situation still feeling comfortable about themselves. At the beginning of this book, the correlation between self-esteem and behaviour was discussed. Adults need to continue to enhance that self-esteem factor through the manner in which they assist children in their acceptable behaviours.

Resolution of conflict is probably one of the most challenging issues for early childhood workers. In a democratic caregiving environment, children are respected and valued. All opinions and feelings are considered to be worthwhile and are listened to. Children are encouraged to feel a sense of belonging and worth, together with ownership, independence and responsibility. Effective conflict resolution will enhance all of these feelings thus promoting high self-esteem.

Consider the situation described earlier between Maria and Rachel. Maria was directed to 'go and sit inside to wait'. How did this affect her ensuing behaviour? There may have been a different outcome for this situation if the adult had listened to both children and assisted them in deciding what should happen.

When young children feel worthwhile and self-discipline is fostered, then they are more likely to resolve problems independently and acceptably. However, adults have to expect and trust that children will do this in developmentally appropriate ways.

Children's own sense of competence and worth (their self-esteem) together with adult guidance, can assist children towards prosocial responses.

Teaching prosocial behaviour

Indirect methods for effective conflict resolution

Indirect guidance is the management of the space, equipment, materials and people to ensure that an optimum environment is available to the children. It is a way of an adult indirectly setting limits through appropriate equipment and supplementary materials. Responsive adults will plan and set up for conflict-free play prior to children being involved in the experience. They will ensure adequate play space and materials for the particular group of children, or for individuals.

Direct guidance methods for effective conflict resolution

In order to effectively manage children's conflicts the responsive adult will recognise not only the significance of indirect guidance, but also strategies that may be used at the time of the conflict. Consider the communication skills you use when you are in a problem situation with another adult? Hopefully, you express your opinion and you listen to theirs. This is what we want to encourage in children, however it needs to be taught and modelled by adults.

Responsive adults have a role in assisting children in finding more acceptable ways of resolving problems rather than using anti-social behaviour. Anti-social behaviour leads to a situation where there are winners and losers. When someone loses out, self-esteem is affected and power struggles often result.

The adult's role in reinforcing prosocial behaviour:
- setting clear and reasonable limits and explaining in an honest, fair manner
- focusing on positive behaviours and encouraging socially acceptable interactions by using phrases of encouragement
- modelling acceptable behaviours in interactions with children and other adults
- being aware of the goals of behaviour, both for adults and for children, and avoiding power struggles
- using choices and consequences rather than punishment
- involving children in limit-setting.

Children are in particular need of assistance towards prosocial behaviour through our encouragement and nurturing guidance

Helping children to help themselves

Responsive caregivers need to be aware of developmentally appropriate strategies for conflict resolution.

Toddlers
Toddlers are still egocentric and usually at a parallel play stage. This means they find it very hard to share. They find it difficult to put themselves in other people's shoes and understand other people's feelings. Toddlers want it 'my' way.

Responsive adults will be aware of their expectations of toddlers and will model cooperative behaviour themselves, both with children and adults. Conflict resolution should be used between adults, so that it is modelled. Adults need to assist young children in finding a solution, then help them follow conflict resolution skills through.

For example, when Kylie, the caregiver, sees 2-year-old Sam hitting another child with a block that he wants, she could say to him, 'Sam, you could ask for the big block instead of hitting Frank.' Responsive adults will encourage children to talk to each other rather than relying on the adult intervening all the time. When Jeda takes Mona's biscuit, the caregiver could say, 'Mona, tell Jeda you don't like it when she takes your biscuit from you. Say to her, "Jeda, that is my biscuit and I want to eat it".'

Young children want to just react. This is normal as they have not yet developed their conflict skills and we need to help them do this. Skills to resolve disputes acceptably will be taught by responsive adults.

The responsive adult in the above situation will encourage children's prosocial actions when they happen. For instance, after Mona tells Jeda that it is her biscuit, the adult will respond to Mona by saying, 'Mona, you said that to Jeda all by yourself. I bet you feel pleased.'

By doing this, the adult is assisting these young children not only with the strategies to resolve conflict but is also empowering children to do it themselves.

There are times when adults expect too much of young children. Toddlers may find it difficult to verbalise their needs and wants, therefore saying to a young child 'Use your words' may be like asking them to speak an unknown language. Toddlers find it hard to put labels on their feelings in order to express themselves. Additionally, there will be times when they want something just because someone else has it, a very typical toddler behaviour.

Adults need to be careful to not give unacceptable behaviour too much attention otherwise it will be reinforced. A clear and simple statement is usually all that is necessary as a response. Responsive adults will remember that children develop skills to communicate, to share, to resolve disputes and to be with groups of children in their own time, when they are ready.

Preschoolers

As has already been noted, most children between three and six years of age are in Erikson's stage of initiative versus guilt. Preschoolers are more cooperative than toddlers. The peer group is important to them and they care about what other people think. Preschoolers are beginning to show a sense of fairness and have the beginnings of moral development. These children are ready to help take on responsibility for their own behaviour and their own thought processes. Responsive adults will be careful to avoid taking over their decisions and will encourage them to make decisions for themselves.

As described below, adults will assist preschoolers in thinking through situations enabling them to feel a sense of control over their own decisions. Self-esteem, self-worth and enhanced social interactions are promoted using this approach.

Assisting independent problem solving through exploring alternatives

There is a very effective conflict resolution method that can be used to facilitate preschool children's ability to resolve problems themselves that is called 'exploring alternatives'. Responsive adults will help children understand the reasons for a problem, assisting them in identifying and considering options available for resolving the conflict. They can then help children follow through with more acceptable behaviour.

In the 3–5 room, a group of children were playing with a wooden train set. One of the children, Joel, aged three-and-a-half, was having difficulty linking the tracks. When he could not join a piece he threw it away and picked up another piece. The thrown piece of track hit another child. Joel kept throwing bits of track. Margaret, the caregiver, approached Joel and said, 'Joel, it seems like you're really mad because your train set won't fit together. But it is really dangerous to throw the pieces around.' Joel replied, 'But I'm mad they won't fit.' And he showed Margaret how they wouldn't go together. Margaret said, 'I wonder if there is another way of joining the tracks together? Is there something else you could do?' Joel suggested a couple of ways, then Margaret suggested a couple of different ways. By trial and error, together with lots of encouragement from Margaret, Joel began to turn the pieces over and around and then said, 'Yes, I could. Look, it works if I do it this way.' Margaret said, 'So how about you try doing it that way now and I'll come and see how you're getting on in a little while.' Joel and the other children resumed their activity. Their play became constructive and cooperative as they worked together to build the train track with associated buildings.

In this situation Margaret and the children worked together to explore alternatives to Joel's problem.

It is possible to identify five steps for facilitating this 'exploring alternative' process:

Step One: Identifying the problem.

Step Two: Brain storming alternative solutions.

Step Three: Deciding on a solution that is prosocial and acceptable.

Step Four: Ensuring that the decision is clearly understood by all concerned.

Step Five: Suggesting a later time to review the situation.

Responsive caregivers will be aware of each of these steps, using them in an informal manner.

Imagine Le, Kate and Tanya are all playing in the block corner. Kate wants all the long blocks to build a road, and Le and Tanya are punching her in order to stop her taking them. George, the caregiver, steps in and facilitates using the above five steps of the 'exploring alternatives' process.

George quietly kneels down to where the three girls are fighting and says, 'Le, Kate and Tanya, it seems that you three are finding it hard to use the blocks properly.' 'Yes, well you see, Kate is taking all our long blocks' says Le. 'It looks like you want some of the long blocks also, Le,' comments George. 'Yes, I want to finish my house.' 'Well,' says George, 'If you need some to finish your house and Kate feels she needs them all for her road, what can we do?' Kate responds, 'I could just have them.' Le says, 'No.' Tanya then adds, 'I think Kate should go out of the block corner.' To which Le replied, 'Yes, we'll play here by ourselves.'

George quietly intervenes saying, 'It seems like Kate is pretty busy here though. What else could you do?' Kate says, 'I could give them some.' Tanya happily replies, 'Yes, you could!' To which George says, 'It looks like you've worked out what you could do. Kate, what do you think will happen if you let Tanya and Le have some of the long blocks?' Kate happily responds, 'I think we'll keep playing and we can build a road going up to their house.' George then asks, 'Are you okay about that, Le and Tanya? Kate will give you some of the long blocks so that you can use them also? Then you can all stay and build more.' 'Yeah!' agree Le and Tanya. 'Okay' says George, 'I'll come back and see how the road and houses are going after I've read Lam a story.'

Responsive adults will use effective communication skills to facilitate the conflict resolution process. George was able to successfully guide these children through a process of exploring alternatives to resolve their conflict. By doing this he empowered them and helped them feel comfortable with their decision. In this way, they came to a win–win resolution.

The five steps outlined above for resolving conflict through exploring alternatives were used effectively by George. The steps can be identified as:

Step 1: Identifying the problem

Using Step 1, George identified the problem. He quietly knelt down where all three girls were fighting. He said, 'Le, Kate and Tanya, it seems like you three are finding it hard to use the blocks properly.'

He then talked more with them about the problem reflecting their feelings and perceptions.

Step 2: Brainstorming alternative solutions

He then moved to Step 2 when he said, 'Well, if you need to finish your house and Kate feels she needs them all for her road, what can we do?' This was brainstorming. He continued to brainstorm with Kate, Le and Tanya, coming up with ideas. He also said, 'What else could you do?', to encourage them to think more.

Step 3: Deciding on a prosocial solution

An acceptable decision was made so George said, 'It looks like you've worked out what you could do. Kate, what do you think will happen if you let Tanya and Le have some of the long blocks?'

Step 4: Ensuring that the decision is clearly understood

George repeated the decision, saying, 'Are you okay about that Le and Tanya? Kate will give you some of the long blocks so that you can use them also. Then you can all stay and build more.' Le and Tanya agreed to the decision.

Step 5: Suggesting a later time to review the situation

George made sure that he let them know he would come back and talk about it further. So he used Step 5. 'Okay' said George, 'I will come back and see how the roads and houses are going after I've read Lam a story.'

The conflict resolution process

By dividing the process into these five steps, it enables the adult to take a potentially difficult situation and break it down into a simple sequential process. As in the development of other skills, effective conflict resolution takes time and practice. Responsive adults will demonstrate equality and respect through their voice and body, promoting children's self-confidence in their own skills and abilities.

Conflict resolution and effective communication

Listening to children's problems

As discussed in Chapter 7, responsive adults know how to effectively listen to children, acknowledging their feelings and actions through reflective statements. When adults use a reflective statement they are viewing situations from the child's perspective, identifying feelings the child might be having, or expressing.

Even though the adult may be perceptive, one cannot be certain about children's feelings. The adult makes an assumption about the feelings. This means that the initial statement needs to indicate a 'perhaps' factor. In other words, it should be tentatively acknowledging the feeling the child appears to have. Responsive adults will find it a useful practice to say, 'It seems like you're feeling . . . ' In this way, a reflective statement can be used very naturally. Making a statement such as this, has a very different meaning to asking children, 'Are you angry?' The first statement implies acceptance and empathy, whereas the latter is simply expecting an answer that can be purely 'yes' or 'no'.

Talking with children about their behaviour

Responsive caregivers will use 'I' statements to express their own feelings about children's behaviour. It is important for children's affective development that they understand other people have feelings and emotions also. However, until children move out of the egocentric infant stage the feelings of others have little meaning. Once children are at a stage of understanding how their behaviour affects others, then 'I' statements become an appropriate communication skill. An 'I' statement informs children of the effect their behaviour has on others and the reasons for this. An 'I' statement about children's behaviour will consist of the following aspects:

- a simple description of the child's behaviour
- a one or two word statement of the adult's feeling when this behaviour happens
- the reasons why the child's behaviour has this effect on the adult.

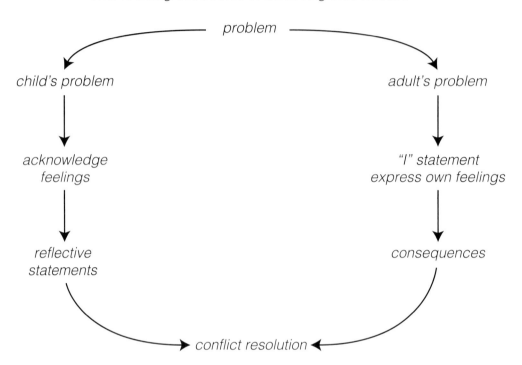

Child's behaviour:
causing problems
for the child

Child's behaviour:
causing problems
for the adult

Who is being obstructed in achieving their needs?

problem

child's problem

adult's problem

acknowledge
feelings

"I" statement
express own feelings

reflective
statements

consequences

conflict resolution

Figure 8 Problem identification

Thus, an 'I' statement will be expressed as follows:
• 'Sally, when you throw the Lego I feel really worried because it may hit someone.'
When adults communicate in this way they will discover how effective 'I' statements are, particularly with preschoolers, in promoting appropriate behaviour.

As stated earlier, conflict resolution skills encourage independent thinking in children. Responsive adults will assist children in finding other, more acceptable ways to resolve problems or disputes, rather than using anti-social behaviour.

Problem ownership

Another aspect of conflict resolution available to responsive adults is that of problem ownership. When adults can identify whose problem a given situation involves, then effective communication skills will more easily fall into place.

There are two factors to identify in problem ownership. The responsive adult will need to decide if a problem is 'mine' or 'yours'. Problem ownership requires the identification of who is being hindered in achieving their needs, and is represented opposite (Figure 8).

Acknowledging problem ownership is not suggesting that one refrains from assisting when it is another person's problem, but it enables the most effective communication to be applied. For example, if Suzy is becoming frustrated because her Lego won't stay together, she owns the problem. The adult could respond with a reflective statement such as, 'Suzy, it seems like you are feeling mad because your Lego won't stay together.'

However, if Suzy's frustration leads her to throw the Lego across the room it affects others and the adult owns the problem. The adult would then respond with an 'I' statement, 'Suzy, when you throw the Lego around, I feel concerned because it might hit someone.'

As it is sometimes difficult to decide who owns the problem, one needs to ask oneself, 'Who is being affected by this situation?' In the first instance, Suzy herself was the one being affected, whereas the adult and the other children were affected by the second situation.

Effective communication enhances prosocial behaviour

Understanding problem ownership will assist responsive caregivers in maintaining effective communication during the conflict resolution process. When adults facilitate the conflict resolution process, they are empowering children in using skills to more effectively socialise in our society. They are encouraging cooperative actions and solutions, whilst promoting non-violent strategies for problem behaviours. A responsive and positive role model is tremendously important for children's affective development. Responsive care-givers who use these methods will be assisting children towards self-discipline and prosocial behaviour.

CHAPTER 12:
Review activities

1 Identify what is meant by prosocial behaviour and describe the adult's role.

2 Identify developmentally relevant factors which may influence effective conflict resolution.

3 Describe the process for effective conflict resolution with preschool age children.

4 Outline the appropriate communication techniques used for conflict resolution. Describe how these are used.

Activities for further learning

1 Consider the following situation and imagine you are the adult responsible for a small group of 3–4-year-olds who really enjoy outdoor play. There is one child who constantly possesses the swings, refusing to allow other children near them. Naturally this causes arguments and physical aggression, with some children no longer wanting to go outside.

(a) Identify how you will encourage more cooperative prosocial behaviour.

(b) Outline the steps you will take to use the technique of exploring alternatives, describing the sequence of questions and a possible solution that may be appropriate.

(c) Observe other adults in adult–child or child–child conflict situations. Note what they are doing and whether or not they reach a successful outcome. Consider what might have been done differently to achieve a win–win outcome.

■ *SECTION IV* ■

RESPONDING WITH GUIDANCE TECHNIQUES

Summary

Limits can be set and carried out in a number of ways, but always the caregiver must be cognisant of children's needs to experiment, mature and develop steadily. Sensible and acceptable limits will reflect an awareness of children's needs at different stages, an understanding of the purposes of behaviour, and anticipation of children's actions. Effective techniques for guiding children within appropriate limits are the use of 'I' messages, to indicate the caregiver's feelings about a particular behaviour, and offering children choices of behaviours and/or activities, so that they feel they can be responsible for their own behaviour.

Applying consequences can be a very effective method of maintaining limits in a democratic and cooperative environment. Aspects to remember are: offer children choices, express yourself in a calm and open manner, relate the consequence to the behaviour, and offer the child the opportunity to choose differently at another time.

These guidance techniques allow children to believe in themselves, their skills and abilities, thereby developing and maintaining a positive self-concept, independence and a sense of responsibility.

■ *S E C T I O N   V* ■

*A*N ENVIRONMENT FOR
EFFECTIVE GUIDANCE

Focus

Children's behaviour is influenced not only by the nature of adult–child interactions, but also by the experiences that are provided for them within an appropriate environment. Realistic expectations of developmental abilities, together with sensitive structuring of the environment, indirectly promote responsible and effective guidance.

$$\boxed{13}$$

Age-appropriate planning

After studying this chapter, the reader will be able to identify reasonable developmental expectations for children's behaviour in various age/stage groups. The importance of planning the environment to facilitate effective guidance for each age/stage grouping will be discussed.

By knowing some general characteristics of infants, toddlers and preschool-aged children, responsive caregivers will provide the optimum environment to guide children's appropriate behaviour and learning, through planned and incidental play experiences. These characteristics will influence caregivers' expectations of children, directly affecting the type and number of experiences which will be provided. This is known as Developmentally Appropriate Practice, where experiences and expectations are not only age-appropriate, but also individually appropriate.

Developmental characteristics of children

Frequently actions that caregivers may identify and respond to as misbehaviours are related to developmental characteristics and skill acquisition in early childhood. The responsive and effective caregiver will provide warm, affectionate and supportive interaction for *all* ages and stages, acknowledging that it is necessary to differentiate some characteristics of key ages/stages.

Infants are in what Piaget calls the 'sensorimotor stage' when they are learning through handling objects, moving about, exploring with hands, body, tongue, ears and eyes. They are also going through a period of attachment and may experience separation anxiety when left in day care. As is described in Chapter 5, infants are developing trust in their caregivers and their environments, requiring caregivers to respond quickly to their cries of distress with reassuring support. Infants need to be held, and to be talked with about what is happening and what is about to happen.

Play involving adults will be interactive and reciprocal so that infants are played with, rather than at. For instance, Charlie, the caregiver, may be on the floor with 10-month-old Guy. He and Guy quietly take turns at *Pat-a-Cake* onto each others hands, each is as involved as the other. Infants repond to many different forms of communication, such as facial expressions, singing and talking, in addition to close physical contact.

So, for example, when Charlie is reponding to Guy's cry for food, he will either get down to Guy's level or pick him up, so that they can look directly at each other. Charlie will gently reassure Guy that his food is coming, perhaps singing to him or rocking him in a pram while he prepares it.

Language is interesting to infants so caregivers should talk with them in a natural, gentle manner, avoiding talking down or using baby talk such as 'you're my little didum itsy bitsy bobsie wobsie' or 'dum, dum, din, din time'. However, responsive caregivers will playfully and respectfully imitate babbling and cooing sounds, responding to infants' early attempts at language while providing them with opportunities for experimenting with their voices.

Encouraging caregivers will provide age-appropriate experiences which are challenging and offer opportunities for infants to practice newly acquired skills. However, they will avoid being expected to entertain all the time, allowing infants opportunities for independent and solitary play. In the situation of Charlie and Guy, Charlie will be aware that Guy needs opportunities for solitary play so he may gently say before moving away: 'Just one more *Pat-a-Cake* Guy, and then I need to go and change Tania's nappy . . . Look, here's a lovely soft doll for you to investigate. She can sit up just like you'.

Caregivers will become familiar with each child's goals and purposes of behaviour, ignoring or limiting the inappropriate behaviours and encouraging appropriate behaviours.

Individual infants have different sleeping, eating and playing patterns, and developmental changes will be taking place rapidly. This makes working with infants very challenging but extremely rewarding.

Toddlers are showing the beginnings of what Erikson calls 'autonomy' as they indicate their own self-awareness and a desire for independence. Caregivers will be supportive of their need for independence by assisting with tasks that may be frustrating, while encouraging children to do as much as possible by themselves. As is discussed in Chapter 10, toddlers need opportunities to explore and test limits, knowing that caregivers will ensure safe boundaries while acknowledging feelings and needs. For example, Karen, aged 2½ years, is throwing water from the water tray onto another child who has taken her funnel. The caregiver, Ilana, notices this and moves across to kneel down beside Karen. Ilana gently, yet firmly, says: 'Karen, it seems like you're angry with Jose for taking your funnel, but the water must stay in the tray. Let's find you another funnel from the basket'.

Children aged 2 or 3 years feel secure in having the same people do things, the same way, day after day. So responsive caregivers will allow children to spend a great deal of time over routines, encouraging their independence and determination to succeed. They will respect children's individual needs and preferences, modelling appropriate behaviours in their own words and actions.

Preschool-aged children are becoming much more social in cooperative play with peers, and like stimulation and extension. They are developing a longer concentration span and may be able to become involved in complex group projects. Caregivers will encourage children's thinking and conversation by asking open-ended questions and following through with appropriate responses as described in Chapters 6 and 7.

Most 4- and 5-year-olds are independent at routine times and like to be involved in routines

Preschoolers enjoy being part of a group and, with guidance, are capable of making appropriate decisions on limits, eating, sleeping and so on, with the needs of other children in mind. Caregivers will invite children to contribute to group discussions and decision making by showing respect for them and their ideas, and by appreciating what they have to offer. Most 4- and 5-year-olds are independent at routine times and like to be involved in routines.

For instance, Leon, the caregiver, has invited his group of 4-year-old children to discuss how they would like to have the room set up for lunch. Leon says: 'I thought it would be good if we changed the furniture in the room around for lunchtime today. What do people think about that idea? What do you think, Jane . . . Peter?' (asking individual children by name). 'Where do you think we should put the tables, Peter?' and so on.

Preschool-aged children are able to be involved in this way because they are less egocentric and moving into the stage that Piaget describes as concrete optional thinking.

Preschool-age children will want opportunities for cooperative small group play

Responsive caregivers will ensure that they acknowledge individual differences between children within the same age group and are aware of this when guiding children's behaviour.

A knowledge of child development allows caregivers to develop certain expectations for the children with whom they are working, so they will plan playrooms, equipment and programs with this knowledge in mind. From their knowledge and experience they will identify expectations for children in physical, social, emotional, cognitive and language development.

Using planning to facilitate guidance of children's behaviour

Appropriate planning of the environment and the experiences offered to children promotes effective guidance of behaviour in an indirect manner. *Indirect guidance* influences children's behaviour through management of the space, the equipment and materials, and the people.

It is the behind-the-scenes work that allows children the opportunity to accept responsibility for their own behaviour, to make decisions and to become independent. All of this is encouraging and fosters a positive self-concept in children. It is children who are feeling discouraged and negative who are more likely to misbehave.

Responsive and effective caregivers will carry out this indirect management by considering the following aspects of their children's environment.

- The physical set-up and space can be arranged appropriate to particular needs and age groups, with equipment which is appropriate to the space and children. For example, infants will need to be given opportunities for sensory exploration, for pulling themselves up and walking around objects. Toddlers require an environment which allows for large muscle activity such as climbing in, out, under and over, and where they can safely be curious and investigate 'why' and 'how'. Preschool-age children will want opportunities for cooperative small group intimate play, an indoor cubby or home corner, and areas for quiet creative activities.

- Appropriate equipment in size and number can be provided according to the group being planned for. Having multiples of equipment will reduce frustrations and power struggles, and will offer children materials that are right for each age/stage group.

- Providing only what is required at a given time, and storing materials you would rather children did not use out of sight, reduces the necessity to continue repeating limits and offers children only acceptable choices.

- A rich and varied program with materials presented in an interesting manner invites children to participate and become involved without needing undue adult intervention.

- The caregiver provides children with an appropriate role model by using equipment and materials in an acceptable manner.

- The daily schedule, and sequence of routines and experiences, can be altered to suit the pace of the children rather than the caregivers. Some flexibility in schedule and routine should be offered to suit individual needs of children. For example, Su-Qum, aged 18 months, is always ready for a sleep at 11.00 a.m. but lunchtime for the infants is at 11.15 a.m. The responsive caregiver may give Su-Qum a small snack before 11.00 a.m., then put her to bed. When Su-Qum wakes she is able to have her lunch and continue playing. A scheduled sequence of events that is followed regularly with only minor changes is most desirable. This offers infants and young children considerable security and knowledge of what to expect.

With this planning and evaluation, guidance will no longer be haphazard and inconsistent giving rise to children feeling discouraged and insecure, but it will be effective and encouraging for both children and caregivers.

CHAPTER 13:
Review activities

1 Using your knowledge and understanding of children's stages of development, identify skills and behaviours which are characteristic of each of the following age groups:
   (a) 0–2 years
   (b) 2–3 years
   (c) 3–5 years.

2 Describe what is meant by 'Developmentally Appropriate Practice'.

3 Identify at least four factors where appropriate planning of the environment will facilitate effective guidance of infants and young children.

4 Describe what is meant by 'indirect guidance'.

Activities for further learning

1 Observe either an infant, a toddler or a preschool-age child in a home setting or an early childhood centre. Consider how the arrangement of furniture, equipment and space makes it easy or difficult for the child to behave appropriately.

2 Identify and list the limits that are being set for the child observed above. Consider whether these correspond with your knowledge of the developmental characteristics of this age group. Reflect on instances where individual needs are being acknowledged.

Recommended reading

Biddulph, S. *The Secret of Happy Children*, Chapter 6.

Dinkmeyer D. & McKay, G. & Dinkmeyer, J. *Parenting Young Children*, Chapter 6.

Hildebrand, V. *Guiding Young Children*, Chapters 3 and 4.

Bredekamp, S. *Developmentally Appropriate Practice in Early Childhood Programs*.

14

WORKING WITH GROUPS: STRATEGIES FOR IMPROVEMENT

Responsive caregivers are providing children with appropriate, positive experiences which will form the building blocks for children's future. A democratic approach to these experiences gives children the opportunity to develop and contribute in a positive way and a democratic approach is a self-esteem enhancing approach. When working with groups of children responsive caregivers will continue to use the foundation of SECRET care. That is, the principles of shared responsibilities, equality, cooperation, respect, encouragement and trust. By doing this, each child in a group will be encouraged to develop a positive sense of self, understanding, and acceptance of other children, and a feeling of trust both in themselves and in others.

Children learn a great deal from adults about being in a group situation. As a leader in a democratic environment the adult is modelling expected behaviours as part of the group. Responsive caregivers are demonstrating respect for others when they listen to children. They are encouraging language skills and the verbalisation of feelings through acknowledging children's comments and non-verbal emotions.

Children learn a great deal from adults about being in a group situation

All adults know how different it is reading a story with just one or two children to reading a story with a large group of children. All sorts of influences and dynamics come into the latter situation causing disruptions, interruptions and distractions to the group. Children's developmental readiness for groups significantly influences how successfully caregivers can guide group situations.

Developmental readiness for groups

Erikson's stages of development outlined in Chapter 3 give us a clue about children's readiness for groups. A young baby is an egocentric being. She believes the world, which is her immediate surroundings, centres on her. It takes time and many varied experiences for babies to develop into more social thinkers and to be able to function successfully within a group situation. Very young children need to be trusting of the adults around them. It is important that they feel acknowledged and have a strong sense of attachment with their carers. So in these early years, the group will be as small as possible giving infants a chance to bond with the caregiver.

From your knowledge of child development, it will be obvious that children who are in Erikson's stage of initiative versus guilt are going to be far more cooperative and imaginative in group experiences than those in the initial two stages. An important factor in working effectively with children is group size. Infants and young children need to be in differing size groups for different purposes. With infants, a group may be as simple as the adult and a child. Whereas with preschoolers, a group may involve at least six or seven children.

Some interesting research has been undertaken on children in groups. Larger groups tend to be overstimulating for any age and quieter children are ignored. It is much harder for children to become involved in a large group than a small one, even when the adult–child ratio is good. A smaller group size encourages more intense and cooperative social behaviour at all ages.

In her research, Berk (1989) suggests that interacting in twosomes is especially conducive in developing early group skills. In the preschool years, small groups of between five to eight members promote more involved and cooperative interactions. Research has also shown that there are cognitive and social advantages to multi-aged groupings in the early years. Children who are developmentally similar interact in ways that are often more positive, more verbal and more likely to evoke cooperative play within the group than just simply children of the same age.

Whatever the group size, children need to feel a part of that group. Children who feel valued and accepted are more likely to contribute positively to the group. For instance Sigrid, aged three-and-a-half, is with a group of peers in their playroom. Sigrid feels accepted, she trusts her caregivers and she knows that they will always follow through. The children are participating in a cooking experience and Sigrid knows from past experience that the caregiver, who has said she may have a turn after Frank, will let her have a turn to stir the cake mix. Thus, Sigrid is far more likely to wait acceptably. In this way, the responsive caregiver assists children's prosocial behaviour. Children's behaviour in groups will not always be prosocial. Their behaviour will be influenced by the various group dynamics existing within that group, particularly in the 3–6-year-old group.

As a responsive caregiver, you will be aware of dominant and passive members of the group. You will observe group members who want to disrupt, and group members who want to control. Children and adults take on different roles in groups. Since groups are different according to their circumstances in which they are held, you will often see different behaviour occurring in different children according to the situation.

In any group there are likely to be children who want to dominate. Their subconscious goal is to control through physical power, aggression or disruptive actions. They don't want to wait until you have finished with someone else. They want your complete attention now. As described in Chapter 8, responsive caregivers will be aware that children such as this respond to responsibility and choice because it gives them a sense of control. Adults need to make it very clear what their expectations of the group are and give children a choice of accepting or not. More often than not, they will accept, particularly children of preschool age. Preschoolers want to be liked and enjoy being part of the peer group. Responsive caregivers will let children know how much they appreciate having them there. However, there may be times when you cannot give these children a choice and they need to be with you for safety and security. This is the ideal time for giving responsibility, thus putting them in control within realistic limits.

Let us imagine you take a group of children to the shop. You may have two caregivers and four children. One child doesn't want to hold your hand and you are already quite a distance from the child care centre. It is important for the child to hold your hand so there is no choice about that. The responsive caregiver may say, 'George, this shopping basket is getting very heavy. You could help me by holding your hand on the shopping basket... That really helps me. Thanks George.' In this way you actually make sure that George holds hands, but in doing it this way you allow him a sense of responsibility.

It is important for caregivers to recognise the power of peer influence on group dynamics and help children to feel it is 'our' group, thus promoting a sense of group identity. For some children, particularly children with special needs, being in a group situation can be overwhelming. These children may need an escape from too much stimulation to a place where they can be secluded with minimal distractions. Responsive adults will provide experiences for young children that will foster appropriate social skills within our cultural framework. Gradual introduction to the concept of being part of the group and the development of decision making for the best interests of the group are all part of pro-social behaviour.

Consider the situation described earlier with Sigrid and Frank. Jack is a caregiver with six children ready for a cooking experience. They are about to stir the cake mix. Before the cooking experience started, Jack sat down with these children and talked about what they were about to do. He talked about mixing the cake and the ingredients they would need. He discussed with them what they could do with the cake afterwards and they all decided they could eat it for morning tea. Jack then talked about the limits that would be necessary for this group experience. He asked the children how they thought they should sit or stand to mix the cake batter. Jack and the children agreed that their hands should stay away from

their mouths and would need washing before they started cooking. Jack reminded them that the spoons they used were for mixing only and must stay away from their mouths until after the mixing had finished. The children and Jack decided that two children could stir the mix at one time, then they could have ten stirs before the next person had a turn. During the group experience, Jack talked and asked questions respectfully. He listened to the children and answered their questions about the cooking simply and honestly. As each ingredient was added, Jack gave a simple reminder using the child's name when it was almost someone else's turn. He would say, 'Sigrid, it's your turn now and when you've had ten stirs, then you can pass it on to Maria.' Jack left it up to the children to remember to pass it on after ten stirs. It was obvious that the children in this group were working very happily and continued the experience in a cooperative manner.

A responsive caregiver will decide the limits with children. By doing this, children feel in control and empowered. They feel responsible and develop self-discipline. Jack and the children were showing respect for each other. Jack was modelling respect with listening and answering skills. As you can see, the most significant factor in this successful group was the responsive caregiver. Responsive caregivers need knowledge of children's developmental levels. They need knowledge about the importance of belonging on both human behaviour and group situations. Responsive caregivers will have effective communication skills, be able to express themselves and listen effectively to children.

Any discussion of children in groups brings forth questions about anti-social behaviours. For example, biting and hitting. As each case depends on the situation there really is no single answer. However, there are a number of factors for responsive adults to consider. Very young children may be biting out of love; that is, they have not yet learnt how to love and hug without using their mouths. Others may be simply exploring and bite out of curiosity because they are still at a very oral stage. It may be that some young children will bite out of anger. It can be the only powerful mechanism they have to express their strong feelings.

Biting, of course, gets an instant reaction from adults which demonstrates just how powerful a behaviour it is. Sometimes

toddlers and preschoolers bite simply as a means of gaining attention, and it really works! Biting provokes an intense reaction, with
adults quickly giving attention to a biting child. Once children
realise the impact this has on a group, it can be a very powerful
attention-getting mechanism.

The general technique to stop biting is to prevent it through
anticipation where possible. Responsive adults will anticipate negative behaviours and so are able to structure their plans differently
to compensate for this. Sometimes however, biting does occur
unexpectedly and when it occurs, it needs to be dealt with firmly
but kindly, without fuss. A useful mechanism is to redirect the
behaviour into something acceptable to bite. The caregiver may
say, 'It looks like you're feeling really mad. I can't let you bite Linda
but you can bite this rubber ring.' You will find more information
about redirection in Chapter 10 of this book.

Other techniques to deal with anti-social behaviour such as this
will depend on the origin of that behaviour. Adults who respond
to the particular need of individuals within the group can more
effectively deal with challenging group behaviour. The adult has
a role in encouraging prosocial behaviour within a group by
ensuring the following:

- Establishing a self-esteem enhancing environment within a
  democratic atmosphere
- Listening to children and encouraging children to listen to each
  other
- Asking open-ended questions to promote children's thinking
- Valuing each group member and being aware that children with
  special needs are more similar than they are different
- Avoiding 'taking over' from children or interfering with child-
  ren's thinking
- Role modelling appropriate behaviours themselves
- Being aware of the necessary limits and assisting children
  towards behaving within those limits
- Enhancing the self-esteem of each group member.

In a self-esteem enhancing and democratic environment, both
children and adults will feel respected and valued. An individual's
opinion and feelings will be considered in a positive manner.
Responsive adults will be aware that children need to feel a sense

of belonging and worth, a sense of ownership and control, and a sense of competence. Effective groups can enhance each of these aspects thus forming the basis for promoting self-esteem.

Group decision making

Group decision making is demonstrated when the responsibility for what goes on within a particular group is shared by the members of that group. Thus, group decision making will enhance a child's sense of competence and worth. It is important to recognise that responsive caregivers will not expect infants to be actively involved in group decision making; however adults will be role modelling important processes. Some strategies for group decision making are appropriate to use with small groups of older toddlers' but adults will need to acknowledge the influence of toddlers' egocentricity and their desire for autonomy. Decision making which is shared by all really does enhance prosocial behaviour because children feel empowered by a sense of ownership, taking satisfaction in being valued for their contribution.

Responsive adults will use either incidental or formal group discussions as an effective method of developing self-discipline and promoting responsible behaviour. Chapter 12 on conflict resolution illustrates that it is also a useful strategy for assisting children in disputes.

Responsive caregivers will always take advantage of teachable moments. For instance, two children are arguing over the bikes. Rather than just take the bikes away, the responsive caregiver will discuss what else the children could do. In other words, adults will be able to quickly and spontaneously go through conflict resolution strategies: 'It looks like you and Daniel are finding it hard to decide whose turn it is on the bike, Gino ... What do you think you can do about it?'

Let the children suggest some alternatives ...

'So, you're both happy to let Gino ride around the path once, and then you'll have a turn Daniel? ... Okay, it sounds like you can have your ride Gino, and then Daniel will have his ride ... I'll come and see how you're enjoying it after I've pushed Alexi on the swing.'

The five steps of identifying the problem, exploring alternatives, coming to a decision, repeating the decision and taking time to re-evaluate are all able to be done spontaneously. Then at the end of the process the caregiver can add, 'Isn't it great that you can sort it out yourselves?' Thus children are allowed to experience a sense of control over their own behaviour.

Group decision making is a method of assisting children solve their problems through their own group processes. It involves awareness of group dynamics and effective communication. Above all, it requires a belief in children's ability for creative thinking and self-discipline.

Responsive caregivers will provide children with opportunities and time to experiment and question. When provided with these opportunities, young children have an enormous capacity to think through problems and come up with very appropriate solutions.

Preschool age groups

The process of group decision making with preschool age children can be facilitated by caregivers with small or large groups of children. Decision making will obviously be more effective with group sizes which enable each child the opportunity to talk and be heard, to listen and to question. Caregivers may either use a formal planned group time or spontaneous incidents, as described earlier, to facilitate group discussion.

When interacting with a group, the adult's communication skills are important, as are the values of mutual respect, social equality and cooperation. The following is the sequence for facilitation which can be used in group decision making.

- *The introductory time*

Recognise the power of peer influence, helping the children to understand that it is 'our' group and to feel a sense of group identity. When a number of children are involved it is important to decide on things that are best for the group as a whole.

Let children know that you care about what each of them has to say, but remind them that it is hard to hear when lots of people talk at once.

Invite children to contribute ideas and to be involved in decision making by showing respect for them and their ideas, and appreciating what they have to offer.

Before talking about problem situations use encouragement. Discuss the positive things that have been happening and describe children's appropriate behaviours. You may say something like, 'It looked like you really enjoyed playing outside when the sun was shining today. Isn't it nice that it stopped raining.' Then you can identify some of the children who were happily playing, prior to talking about the problem behaviour that you may wish to discuss.

- *Sorting out the problem*

Whether it is just two children or a larger number in the group, clearly put forward the problem to the children, presenting it in a concise and warm manner that they can understand. If you go into unnecessary details, it will just distract children and confuse them. Ask them for their ideas if you think it is appropriate. Show them that you really value their opinion by listening carefully to what they say. Reflective listening may be appropriate to find out what a child really means. So you could use, 'It seems like you're saying...'

Guide the children's decision making through careful questioning and statements, so that they are learning to anticipate events or happenings, and can foresee the consequence of decisions that they make. You might say, 'What do you think would happen then?' You need to be careful to not allow permissiveness and chaos to take over, but remember your value of freedom within limits.

If children find it hard to reach agreements about their problems, you need to consider fair methods to help them in their decision making. Voting is not appropriate, as children need to learn to cooperate and to find ways to reach a consensus agreeable to all. Remember, as with conflict resolution you are looking for 'win–win'. You as the responsible adult need to ensure that you set and maintain limits. Thus, the adult may sometimes need to make the decision for children.

Make sure that all children are aware of the decision that has been agreed to, by very clearly repeating it back to the group. For example, you could say, 'So it sounds like we have decided to . . .' You may also include in this statement consequences for children who are not wanting to cooperate after they have agreed to the decision. For example, 'So we've decided that we do need to sit quietly for a story. What shall we do if someone still keeps being noisy?'

Help children decide on an appropriate logical consequence for this behaviour as in Chapter 11, and again ensure they understand it by repeating it as you did when using 'Exploring alternatives' in Chapter 12.

As in 'Exploring alternatives' talk about when you will re-evaluate. Decide when you will return to see how things are going. Let children know that there is always an opportunity to change any decision that they have made.

Concluding your group decision making

Four and 5-year-olds do want to cooperate when they are treated fairly and respectfully by adults. Offer children encouragement when they are making their decisions. Focus on how responsible and independent they feel when deciding things for themselves by using communication skills that acknowledge children's feelings or express your own feelings. By enabling children to take responsibility for their behaviour the responsive caregiver will be reinforcing prosocial behaviour.

As has been stated previously, group decision making can be implemented with small or larger groups of children, and in a formal or spontaneous manner. The responsive caregiver will always be aware of promoting a self-esteem enhancing environment.

CHAPTER 14:
Review activities

1 Describe the characteristics of the following three stages as outlined by Erikson. Considering the influence of these characteristics on the behaviour of children in group situations:
0–18 months
18 months–3 years
3 years–6 years.

2 Describe the influence group size may have on prosocial behaviour and group interactions.

3 Outline the process for group decisions which promote prosocial behaviour in preschool children.

Activities for further learning

1 Consider a time when you, as an adult, were part of a group experience. Describe the dynamics occurring within the group and the various roles 'played' by group members. Identify your role within this group.

2 Outline the steps you may take to promote group decision making in the following situation: The block corner in the kindergarten room was a very busy place. Four children were constructing an airport using some new blocks that had been introduced. Some of the children were playing carelessly with these new blocks, deliberately banging the sides together. The caregiver was concerned about their lack of respect for the new equipment and feared that someone may get hurt. The caregiver wanted to use the ideas of each of the children in deciding what should be done, but was unsure of the appropriate process. How would you manage this situation?

■ SECTION V ■

AN ENVIRONMENT FOR EFFECTIVE GUIDANCE

Summary

The environment in which an infant or child functions will influence particular types of behaviour. Responsive and effective caregivers will be aware of differing needs and developmental expectations of infants, toddlers and preschool-age children when considering guidance and planning programs. These caregivers will plan developmentally appropriate environments and programs, so facilitating the reinforcement of positive behaviours in children.

■ S E C T I O N   V I ■

Making it work for you

Focus

It takes courage to begin to understand ourselves in order that we may understand and respond appropriately to others. However, by doing this we are more likely to develop and maintain positive relationships with our families, friends, children, co-workers and other adults.

By creating an atmosphere based on mutual respect, trust, cooperation and responsibility, children and adults will grow in self-reliance, self-esteem and self-discipline.

The principles outlined in *Understanding Children* are universal to all democratic relationships. Chapters 15 and 16 identify the specific challenges of implementing these ideas in our relationships with children, while Chapters 17 and 18 relate the democratic values to the wider early childhood environment of co-workers and parents.

In order to make this approach work for them, readers are encouraged to reflect on their own values in Chapter 19.

15

*C*ULTURAL DIVERSITY WITHIN A DEMOCRATIC APPROACH

The self-esteem enhancing principles outlined in this book are based on current knowledge and thinking about children's behaviour. These principles have not always been widely acknowledged. The principles are universal to all democratic relationships and reflect the belief in the equality of people regardless of age, background, culture or religion. They involve the rights of the child as well as the adult.

Principle Two of the United Nations Declaration on the Rights of the Child, 1959, states, 'The child shall enjoy special protection and shall be given opportunities and facilities by law and other means to enable him to develop physically, mentally, emotionally, spiritually and socially in a healthy and normal manner and in conditions of freedom and dignity. In the enactment of laws for this purpose, the best interest of the child shall be the paramount consideration.'

Although we have regulations to ensure this necessary and appropriate protection of children when in group care, caregivers also need to be sensitive to children's home environments.

Australia was criticised in a 1994 UNICEF report for not having nationwide laws against physical punishment of children in schools or at home. In countries where corporal punishment has been banned in the home, there has been adequate training of parents and educators in alternative modes of non-punitive behaviour management. The traditional autocratic approach in which punishment is decided upon by the adult and the adult is boss, leads to increased feelings of inferiority and children lacking responsibility and self-discipline. Some people believed that if you punished or humiliated a child enough, that would be all that was needed to change behaviour. Responsive adults are aware that this approach only emphasises the belief that being an adult means to be superior, powerful and to do as you wish. Additionally, it limits children in their capacity and decision making because the adult does all the deciding, using punishment as a means of suppressing unacceptable behaviour.

Accepting and becoming accustomed to a different guidance approach can create a discipline dilemma for some adults. Child care staff and parents often unnecessarily devote much of their time and energy to dealing with children's unacceptable behaviour because they are unsure about alternatives to their traditional approach. Unfortunately, this uncertainty and confusion may result in them reverting to an autocratic manner with total control over the child in order to give themselves a sense of security. It is important to keep in mind that both children and adults have rights and we need to learn to respect each other's rights.

Cultural diversity

When we consider the historical perspective of child rearing from generation to generation, it can be seen that different child raising practices flourish across various ethnic groups according to their own values and expectations of children. For thousands of years, parents and children learnt how to raise children through grandmothers and grandfathers, aunts and uncles. These were people who had lived together in that culture for generations.

Some culturally embedded child management practices fit into a different framework from this self-esteem enhancing democratic approach. Particular parents may prefer the use of certain strategies over others. But as a responsive caregiver, your focus must always remain on the needs and rights of all children, with the best interest of the child being paramount.

So different cultural practices may pose a dilemma within a democratic child care setting.

Cross-cultural sensitivity: a case study

Trang, a 20-month-old, is in a homebased care situation where there is also a two-year-old and a three-year-old. Each of these children is active and enjoys outdoor activities. Gwen, the caregiver, structures her program to enable the children to have opportunities for independent gross motor play outside. Trang's parents have stated to Gwen that they want Trang to have layer after layer of clothes on before she goes outside now that the weather is getting cooler as this is their cultural practice. Gwen follows through with this but she observes over a number of days that Trang is running around less than normal and has become unusually dependent on Gwen for play activities. From her knowledge of child development Gwen is aware that children need to have numerous opportunities for independent physical play and should be encouraged towards self-reliance in their activities. She considers Trang's changed behaviour may be a consequence of her tightly layered, restrictive clothing. Gwen is concerned for the child's growth and development, and wants to put Trang into less clothing, but she also acknowledges the parental values and customs.

A situation such as this may create a similar dilemma for you. Responsive caregivers will respect the socio-cultural views on child rearing whilst at the same time maintaining a high quality, developmentally appropriate child care environment. This potential conflict may require a great deal of sensitive communication with the family but the focus should always remain on the best interests and rights of the child.

It is important to assess one's own personal values in relation to other people, whether it is the children who will be in your care, the adults with whom you are working or the parents. As caregivers focusing on the needs of the child, it is important to acknowledge that the parent is also the client, not just the child. Responsive adults are careful to make decisions after consulting parents about family beliefs; however individual decisions and attitudes will be based largely on the values you hold. As a caregiver, it is important to assess your own values, your own upbringing, your philosophy of life, your family dynamics and education. Each of these will be reflected in your program and in your relationships with others.

Values are the 'oughts' or 'shoulds' that guide our actions. Many values are unconscious or unknown until a trigger brings them to the surface. Adults have been acquiring values all their lives from family, friends and the community. An individual's own unique life experiences lead that person to have particular values, so it follows that others with different life experiences and family backgrounds may have varying values. We need to appreciate parents' different values, being sensitive to their needs or beliefs whilst maintaining our knowledge of appropriate practice for children.

Sensitivity to cultural diversity is extremely important. A responsive caregiver does not need to give up his or her beliefs, but will assess the differences from the parent's point of view also. Adults who effectively communicate with each other will be able to come to a position of negotiation and compromise. A meaningful approach to cultural diversity comes from learning about other value systems such as how another person's culture may differ from your own. Communicating effectively with each other will contribute to a better understanding of, and increased sensitivity to, alternative beliefs that others may have.

In a democratic caregiving environment, if others do not wish to accept our values, that is their right. At times responsive caregivers may need to re-examine their own values to consider whether or not they wish to continue holding these. Value orientations are hard to change but can be adapted given adequate reasons and understanding of the situation. Responsive adults will consider the rights of children, equality of worth and mutual respect between caregivers and parents, adults and children.

A meaningful approach to cultural diversity comes from learning about other value systems

Respect and acceptance of others' rights to differing views and willingness to discuss conflicts are essential. Responsive adults will acknowledge and resolve differences in a manner that ensures all people will feel accepted for who and what they are.

CHAPTER 15:
Review activities

1 Describe why corporal punishment, such as smacking, is inappropriate. Relate this to your knowledge of the factors influencing a self-esteem enhancing environment.

2 Suggest how a responsive caregiver will behave when confronted by someone with different beliefs. Outline the communication skills that will be necessary in this situation.

3 Which democratic principles are responsive adults demonstrating when they acknowledge another person's different beliefs and values?

Activities for further learning

1 Consider your own cultural background and that of people from other cultures. Identify some expectations of children's behaviour that your parents had that may have been different from parents in another culture. Discuss these expectations and give reasons for the differences. Consider how you can incorporate diverse cultural expectations into a self-esteem enhancing approach.

2 Read the United Nations Declaration on The Rights of the Child. Identify how an early childhood professional can implement these principles within his or her program.

3 A parent approaches you with concerns about disciplining her child. The parent believes she needs to smack her child to promote more acceptable behaviour. As a responsive adult, how can you be supportive of the parent whilst maintaining your belief about the rights of the child? Discuss the alternative methods of encouraging prosocial behaviour you will offer, giving reasons for your suggestions.

CHAPTER

$$16$$

Using the Principles

After studying this chapter, the reader will be able to follow certain principles for caregivers based on a responsive and effective caregiving approach.

The techniques of democratic and effective caregiving, seen in isolation, may appear disjointed and unrelated to the wider caregiving atmosphere. Therefore, a final identification of principles based on learning from previous chapters may assist caregivers in using their knowledge.

Even though you may have developed relevant skills it can be difficult putting them into practice, particularly if others around you show little interest in change.

Principles for responsive and effective caregiving

Develop confidence in your new approach

Learning new skills, or reinforcing existing ideas in responsive and effective caregiving requires patience and persistence. Take one step at a time by practising one new idea at a time, allowing yourself to develop confidence in using guidance techniques successfully. Although some skills may seem artificial at first, with practice you will adapt them to your own style.

Change your own behaviour

Children's behaviour can most effectively be influenced by changing your own behaviour, and using a positive and encouraging approach.

Encourage positive behaviours by modelling those yourself and by showing appreciation to children.

Showing confidence in children will assist them in developing a positive self-concept and trust in their interpersonal relationships.

Demonstrate a democratic approach

Democratic relationships assist everyone to become more responsible and more capable. Always show respect and be honest with children, parents and other caregivers, but also be tactful.

Democratic procedures are based on equality and mutual respect. They allow children to make choices within acceptable limits. Encourage this decision making but be careful not to offer too many choices or to expect children to make too many decisions.

Demonstrate responsive communication

Infants and young children need to be listened to in a sensitive manner and to feel understood. Reflective listening acknowledges children's feelings while showing acceptance and understanding.

Caregivers need to be able to communicate their feelings to children and to each other. 'I' messages express our feelings in a respectful and non-judgemental manner.

Respond to inappropriate behaviour according to its purpose

Most inappropriate behaviour has a social purpose related to the four goals of misbehaviour. By responding appropriately and consistently to the misbehaviour, you can guide children's behaviour.

All children seek attention. However children who are misbehaving for attention should be ignored when possible and given attention for positive behaviour.

Assist young children to accept limits by discussing the limits with them and by involving them in deciding appropriate limits, choices and consequences.

Withdraw from power struggles using consequences instead of punishment. Always follow through and be consistent with consequences.

Children who are showing revenge may hit, bite or hurt other children, however, retaliation only stimulates further revenge. Never hit, bite or physically punish a child. Use consequences and redirection instead.

Always encourage children. Children displaying inadequacy may not be unable, rather they may just lack belief in themselves and their ability, or they may not yet have developed the particular skills. Accept children's mistakes while encouraging appropriate behaviour.

Believe in yourself

Responsive and effective caregivers will demonstrate democratic values not only with children but also with adults, and understand one another's behaviour.

By working and sharing ideas together, caregivers are able to encourage one another as cooperative members of a team.

Be willing to share your successful and unsuccessful caregiving techniques with peers. Accept yourself and believe in yourself as an effective and responsible caregiver.

CHAPTER 16:
Review activities

1 Consider your methods of guiding children's behaviour and identify which of the principles outlined in this chapter you are using.

2 Identify the principles which you consider to be most important for you and describe why this is so.

3 Identify the principles which you find most difficult to use. Reflect on these and practise their appropriate use.

Activities for further learning

1 Identify an aspect of children's behaviour where you feel you are having difficulty using effective guidance. Reflect on the problem and then consider how you could use responsive and effective caregiving principles. You will need to:
(a) identify the problem
(b) work out which technique is appropriate to the problem
(c) decide on an alternative response to more effectively guide the behaviour.
Next time you are faced with this behaviour follow through your alternative response.

Recommended reading

Balson, M. *Becoming Better Parents*, Chapter 7.
Biddulph, S. *The Secret of Happy Children*, Chapter 8.

17

CARING FOR THE CARERS

After studying this chapter, the reader will be able to identify and understand ways of applying democratic principles to the effective functioning of an early childhood centre. In addition, you will be able to understand and accept the behaviour of other adults, and to respond in a sensitive and appropriate manner to them.

Parents and caregivers who feel respected and trusted by others, who are non-judgemental in their words and actions, will feel supported and welcomed. In order to offer this support and respect, caregivers need to feel okay about themselves and to accept responsibility for their own behaviour.

A democratically organised early childhood centre

We are each responsible for our own behaviour, and need to develop techniques which help us as individuals in our relationships with others. We cannot make other people change their behaviour, but we can make the decision to change our own behaviour, our feelings and our beliefs.

In order to develop effective relationships with others, it is necessary to begin by feeling okay about ourselves and what we do, including our work. Parents, the community and even staff themselves, often have unrealistic expectations of the role of early childhood workers. Staff are expected not only to interact with numbers of children (observing, planning, caring and providing appropriate experiences) but also to interact with parents (being supportive, reassuring, knowledgeable and a source of referral) and to work cooperatively with their peers. It is no wonder that many staff suffer from burnout! Theses relationships can be represented as a triangle with inter-relating sides as shown in Figure 9. Each side of the triangle is essential to the others in order to maintain balance and equanimity.

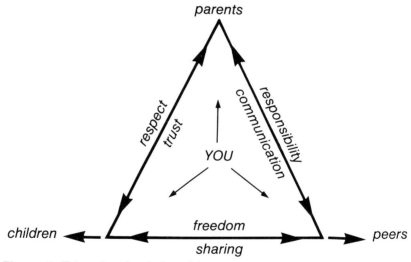

Figure 9 Triangle of relationships

Emotional and physical exhaustion can seriously affect an individual's psychological well-being and impair the ability to relate effectively to people in general. Effective relationships are the foundation of the caregiver's work.

Working with children during their formative years is incredibly important, and quality child care is vital to the community

Effective communication and democratic relationships are the foundation of the caregiver's work

and society as a whole. Caregivers can recognise the value of one another and encourage each other in this essential task.

A democratically organised early childhood centre will enhance staff feelings of positive self-esteem and high task value. It will have the following features:

Mutual respect → for one another's feelings and values.

Equality → of worth. Each adult is of equal value and can make equally worthwhile contributions.

Trust → in one another to reduce conflicts and grievances and to carry out responsibilities.

Cooperation → by offering and encouragement, sharing ideas and supporting one another.

Freedom → to contribute to decision making by having frequent and purposeful staff meetings.

Again, each of these aspects is important to the support and development of the others. Caregivers are able to model behaviour which is cooperative, responsible and encouraging.

Goals of adult behaviour

In order to interact effectively and supportively with other adults, it is important to understand behaviour and respond appropriately. If we are able to begin to comprehend ourselves, we can then relate to others and show an understanding of their behaviour. Just as children have goals of behaviour, so too do adults. We have simply learned to be more circumventive and evasive in achieving our goals. Consistent inappropriate or negative behaviour needs to be understood and responded to in the context of its purpose. Purposive behaviour can have positive rather than negative goals, however it is usually the negative goals that cause concern, discouragement and deteriorating relationships. As with children's behaviour, the goal can be identified by the feeling you have as a consequence of the person's behaviour.

Attention
As with children, the attention-seeking adult also desires to *keep people busy or to be noticed*. This may be the caregiver who is always losing things and asking other people to search for them. Others *feel annoyed* by it, but respond to be helpful. However, is it helpful? If reinforced, behaviour such as this is then repeated in a variety of ways and in different situations. The attention-seeking adult may be a parent, who constantly interrupts you when you are talking with a child or another parent. It is not all that important, but you feel annoyed.

In order not to reinforce this annoying behaviour you may ignore it, thus not giving attention, or you may quietly let them know that you will give them time when you can.

Power
Adults who subconsciously *desire to control and to let others know that they are superior* often find passive, non-obvious ways to achieve

their goal. It may be that they continually arrive back late from lunch, thus keeping someone else from taking their much needed break on time. Possibly it will be the caregiver or parent who always believes that others should do things her 'better way', where there is no room allowed for cooperation or negotiation. Those experiencing this behaviour will *feel threatened, angry and challenged*.

People who are using power for a negative purpose may begin to change their behaviour if they experience consequences without a power struggle. However, if the recipients of the behaviour allow themselves to become involved in an argument or battle, then the person's purpose of power and control is achieved. A person who is always late back from lunch may just have to always take last lunch break (this is the consequence of their inappropriate behaviour). That way they are not controlling anyone else's break.

A successful way to solve problems between adults is through effective communication and identification of problem areas. 'I' messages are very appropriate and also show respect for other people. The problem of people always coming back late from lunch may be brought up at a staff meeting with an 'I' message. For example: 'When people are kept from having their proper lunch break I feel really concerned because it creates stress and unfair pressures'. Then all staff will be involved in discussions and decisions about it.

Revenge

There may be parents or caregivers who will *make hurtful comments to others, or set out to ensure that another person's well thought out program does not work*. Their actions may be small, and alone they may be insignificant, but a repeated pattern of this behaviour will be very *destructive and hurtful* to others. It is the discouraged person whose subconscious purpose is to be recognised through revengeful behaviour, and this person will need encouragement and support from others rather than retaliation. It will always be difficult and courageous to avoid feeling hurt if you are the recipient of this revengeful behaviour from a discouraged person. Staff need to be aware of the need to be supportive and encouraging of one another.

Some parents may display this goal to caregivers if they have feelings of guilt and disappointment at not being home with their children. Discouraged people, such as these, start feeling more comfortable about themselves when reassured and encouraged by others who are non-judgemental and have not allowed themselves to be hurt through the goal of revenge.

Assumed inadequacy

This describes a *helpless manner that is not organically caused* but which a person adopts for reasons they may not understand. An adult may become so very discouraged and so lacking in belief in themselves that they just give up. Those around that person *feel helpless and unsure as to how to respond*. This should not be confused with a power struggle where the inadequate person's purpose is to control. In that circumstance one would feel angry, resentful and perhaps threatened.

Assumed inadequacy is hard to deal with, but fortunately is not a common problem. It may be seen in a parent who is just ready to give up or who expresses the belief that she just cannot accept any responsibilities. Caregivers will respond in small and unobtrusive ways by offering encouragement and support without undue attention.

Democratic caregivers

In a democratic caregiving environment, caregivers will be aware of the goals of their own behaviour and the manner in which they are interacting with children, parents and staff. Caregivers will make their own decisions about how they will change their behaviour, based on their understanding of themselves and others, and the skills that they have developed. Democratic caregivers will communicate with respect and sensitivity for others, using effective communication skills of reflective listening and 'I' messages.

This approach to adult relationships is synonymous with that outlined earlier for understanding and responding to children's behaviour.

CHAPTER 17:
Review activities

1 Identify five aspects of democratic caregiving which can be applied to the effective functioning of an early childhood centre.

2 Describe the behaviour expressed by each of the four goals of negative behaviour.

3 Identify four effective ways to respond to negative behaviour and reinforce appropriate behaviour.

Activities for further learning

1 Ask yourself each of the following questions, consider your answer and what you would do about it.
   (a) Is your goal to control everyone else or to be an effective leader?
   (b) Do you often desire attention and want to keep others involved with you?
   (c) Do you try to get back at others or to humiliate them?
   (d) Do you expect other people to take on your responsibilities as well as their own, or to do things for you that you could do with a little effort?

2 Imagine you are the coordinator of an early childhood centre that functions on democratic principles and you need to display a poster about your centre's philosphy. Design a poster with a brief written statement.

3 Find out what courses local colleges or community centres are offering, and participate in a course or seminar on Effective Communication or Interpersonal Relationships.

Recommended reading

Schnebly, L. *Out of Apples.*

$$18$$

PROGRAMS FOR PARENTS

After studying this chapter, the reader will develop an aware-ness of the importance of responding to parent needs, and will be able to identify some reasons for planning and conducting programs of particular interest to parents. The reader will be able to plan an effective and responsive parent program by following the sequence outlined in this chapter

Support for parents

Early childhood workers are aware that it is not possible to emphasise too strongly the significance of parenthood in our society. The interaction of parent and child within the environ-ment is evident in every child's life. Each aspect interconnects at every point of their life together, creating a unique lifestyle for each family. It is assumed by some people that the birth of a baby transforms individuals into caring mothers and fathers with appropriate parenting skills. However, the ability or desire to effectively nurture and care does not appear automatically, and new mothers and fathers often neither wish to, nor are able to, model their behaviour on the parenting approach of their own parents.

The changes towards a more democratic society that was discussed in Section I, and the evolution of nuclear and single parent families, have created new pressures on families today. Although each of these families is individual with differing needs, there are certain underlying patterns which can be observed and relevant principles and skills which can be applied to these various parenting situations. The principles and skills are similar to those outlined in early chapters of this book.

If we are to take seriously the view that society's future is in our children, then it becomes society's and our concern. The government, churches, schools, early childhood centres and so on, have a responsibility to develop programs which teach these principles and assist parents to develop skills that they may use towards positive relationships with their children. Additionally, it is society's and our responsibility to make available support systems for parents in need.

Early childhood workers are in a unique position of closeness with parents and will learn a great deal from them, but at the same time have an enormous amount to give themselves. It is necessary to establish and keep open reciprocal lines of communication and trust between yourself and parents. This two-way interaction assists parents to feel comfortable and secure with the persons who are caring for their children, and conversely allows the caregivers the opportunity to relate ideas, meaningful events and incidental happenings with the parent. Caregivers will use this close relationship to support parents and to gather information about their needs.

Parents and early childhood workers will work together on planning supportive and relevant activities to meet their needs. Many parents are requesting programs in skills and knowledge, designed to maintain and extend responsible and sensitive relationships with their children. It has been shown that these programs are most effective if offered when parents have young families, and when they are adapted for particular groups and flexible to individual needs.

Planning a responsive and effective parent program

The steps to be considered are listed in Figure 10.

Caregivers may be aware of what *they* consider the needs of parents to be, however before offering a program of activities for them, it is important that *parents* be given the opportunity to identify their specific needs. This can be achieved through informal discussions, questionnaires, newsletters and so on. Caregivers can find out what the parents consider their needs to be, what they would like a program to focus on, and what role they would like the leader or caregiver to have.

Step 1

A friendly, social session to introduce the concept of a parenting program will provide a non-threatening opportunity for parents and caregivers to discuss their requirements and share ideas.

Once ideas have been clarified and the needs of the parent group are established, the caregiver or leader will develop a specific focus for the program. From this, objectives will be established in order that parents and caregivers are certain as to what the program is designed to do.

Step 2

A structured parent group will require a leader who is able to support and motivate the group, allowing effective learning and interactions to take place. It is the leader's attitudes, skills and knowledge that will influence the interactions within the group, and thus the value of the experience for the participants.

Step 3

Leading a parent group can be seen as an extension of the democratic principles the reader will have already developed for effectively and positively caring for children. Parents will be allowed the opportunity to acknowledge their own beliefs and values, and will be accepted for themselves. It is each participant's responsibility and choice to accept or reject what is being offered. Clearly the principles of respect, equality, trust and cooperation are particularly relevant in a group such as this.

1 ↓	*Identify the needs of the parent group*	→	Informal talks, letters, questionnaires, discussions, social nights
2 ↓	*Decide on the objectives for the program*	→	Gather all the information from 1 and work out the focus
3 ↓	*Explore ways to carry out the objectives*	→	Will you have a guest speaker, videos, staff panels, parent-led discussions?
4 ↓	*Allocate and advise dates, times and locations in advance*	→	Use noticeboards, newsletters, informal talks and so on
5 ↓	*Check out any major problems that may prevent participation*	→	Discuss with parents the most convenient times, days and so on
6 ↓	*Carry out the planned program*	→	Have you thought about supper, heating, locking the building, comfortable chairs?
7 ↓	*At the end of the program ask parents to evaluate it according to your objectives*	→	Evaluation form, questionnaire, discussion
8 ↓	*Review and consider any further parent programs*	→	Gather information from evaluations and assess value of program in terms of objectives
9 ↓	*Share your knowledge and success with others*	→	Be satisfied with the supportive and caring role you have played

Figure 10 Planning a responsive and effective parent program

Steps 4 and 5

Parents have their own needs to consider as well as many commitments. If the caregiver wishes to encourage as many parents as possible to participate in a parent activity, then parents need to be given adequate notification of events to enable their own planning to take place. Caregivers will talk with individual parents about the most suitable day and time, as well as finding the most convenient location for all concerned.

Caregivers need to ensure that parents are clearly informed by, for example, newsletter or notice board, to allow time to organise themselves. Further discussion may take place to consider problems such as babysitting arrangements which would preclude parents from participating. In order to be encouraging and supportive the early childhood centre committee or staff could organise to provide child care during parent activities.

Step 6

The real value of parent programs lies not just in the knowledge gained from principles and skill development, but also in the group unity and respect developed for one another through sharing and learning together. A successful parent program will be one that is encouraging of parents, rather than producing feelings of anxiety or guilt for what they are doing 'wrong'. Participating group members are able to develop increased confidence in their own skills and a belief in themselves as effective parents.

This enthusiasm and confidence is often shared with non-participating parents who then request a repeat program. So the richness of the experience will be transferred to others, according to their needs.

A particular situation, which requires a specific program for parents, is in the event that caregivers decide to change or adapt their own approach to relationships and behaviour. In these circumstances it is particularly important that an information-sharing session is held with parents. When your behaviour and attitudes towards something or someone change, those around you may become confused and unsure of what you are doing, if they do not understand. Thus you need to be available to provide support and information. There are a number of strategies that may be used in this situation. For example, staff of an early childhood centre may invite a guest speaker to give a short talk to provide an informed knowledge base to parents, or run a series of workshops on the issues for staff and parents.

When parents have attended a structured program, the caregiver or leader will gather feedback on the success or value of the program in meeting the needs of the group. This evaluation will allow for future planning of programs, and also enable clarification of any aspects. The participants in any program are the most important people, so leaders need to be open and responsive to their suggestions and ideas.

Steps 7 and 8

After undertaking the planning and carrying through this program, the leader will be able to acknowledge the role that such programs have in supporting parents and contributing to the effective functioning of the family as a nurturing unit. This acknowledgement of satisfaction and value can be very encouraging to caregivers.

Step 9

Early childhood workers are expected, and wish to, work closely with families, providing not only for the children but also their parents. This takes time and energy, and may increase the stress load on a group of people already under pressure. However effective caregivers will be supportive and encouraging of each other. They will feel comfortable with themselves, believing in their own abilities, and will thus convey a reassuring message to others around them.

To assist caregivers or leaders with setting up a responsive and effective parent program, Figure 10 illustrates the processes which have been outlined in this chapter.

CHAPTER 18:
Review activities

1 Identify two reasons why today's parents may consider attending a parenting skills program. What societal factors have influenced this?

2 Suggest why an early childhood centre is ideally suited to offering a parent education program.

3 Outline the nine steps involved in planning and implementing a successful parent program.

4 Identify three important attributes of an effective leader in a parent program.

Activities for further learning

1 Compile a questionnaire designed to identify parent needs for parent programs. Distribute this to a group of parents in an early childhood centre.

2 From the above questionnaire design a responsive parent program which will meet these needs.

3 Find out about parenting programs offered within your local community. Make a list of these available to parents.

Recommended reading

Berger, E.H. *Parents As Partners in Education.*

C H A P T E R

$$\boxed{19}$$

A FINAL WORD: VALUES

After studying this chapter, the reader will be aware of the influence of personal values on their interactions with others.

It would be remiss of me to present a book such as this without discussing caregivers' own values, beliefs and the implications this may have for the parents and children with whom they work. For example, I *believe* that groups function most effectively when working with a democratic approach. That is my belief, I am allowed to have it. However, I acknowledge that not everyone will feel the same way about that belief, perhaps because their value systems and cultural backgrounds are dissimilar to mine, or maybe because their unique life experiences led them to a different set of beliefs. It doesn't matter, providing we each respect others' rights to their own set of beliefs.

As caregivers, it is important to assess our values in relation to other people, whether it is the children in our care, adults with whom we are working or parents.

A caregiver's own upbringing, philosophy of life, human development, family dynamics and education, will be reflected in their programs and relationships. Sharing and discussing our beliefs contributes to a better understanding of, and increased sensitivity to, alternative value systems that others may choose to have.

If others do not wish to accept our values that is their right, and at times we need to re-examine our own values to see if we wish to continue with them. However, it is important to acknowledge that we each have a right to our own set of beliefs.

Caregivers are encouraged to consider the cultural backgrounds of children and adults. These have implications for values and belief systems relating to children's behaviour, rights of children, equality of worth and mutual respect between caregivers themselves, or between caregivers and parents. Respect and acceptance of each other's rights to differing views, and willingness to discuss conflicts, are essential. Of direct concern to caregivers is the acknowledgement and resolution of differences, so that all people will feel accepted for who and what they are.

CHAPTER 19:
Review activities

1 Suggest how a caregiver should behave when confronted by someone with different beliefs.

2 Which democratic principles are you demonstrating when you acknowledge another person's different beliefs?

Activities for further learning

1 Play *The Lifeboat* game.

The Lifeboat Game

You are on a luxury cruise ship and have just spent seven wonderful days sailing the South Pacific. All passengers have become well acquainted and most relate well with each other. On your second last night at sea your ship hits a coral reef about 10 kilometres off-shore and immediately begins to sink. The Captain informs you of the following:

▫ You are to divide into three groups.

▫ Each group will have access to one lifeboat.

- Each lifeboat will hold only four passengers so you may have an excess of people.
- Therefore each group will have to decide who can use the lifeboat.

The backgrounds of the people who are needing to go into one lifeboat are:

- a career girl of 19 who is having her first working holiday as a nanny to one 3-year-old child.
- a 25-year-old female who is a single mother of three children under 5 years old. She is on the trip to dry out from drug dependence and alcholism.
- a middle-aged couple (both divorcees) who have just begun a new life together. They have no children, but a dependant invalid parent at home who requires ongoing constant care.
- a 21-year-old male who is paraplegic but can get himself around independently in his wheelchair, or with the help of one other person if there is no wheelchair.

One of the above people cannot be fitted into this lifeboat as it only holds four passengers. If more than four get in, it will capsize and you will all be stranded at sea.

How will you decide who can be in a lifeboat?

What criteria will you use?

Why?

2 Read Schnebly *Out of Apples*, Chapters 1 and 2 and discuss what causes us to have certain values, beliefs and attitudes.

3 Read Ellis and Harper A *New Guide to Rational Living* and discuss with others whether or not we can change our beliefs and attitudes.

Recommended reading

Ellis, A. and Harper, R. A *New Guide to Rational Living*.

Montgomery, B. and Evans, L. *You and Stress*: A *Guide to Successful Living*.

Schnebly, L. *Out of Apples* Chapters 1 and 2.

■ *SECTION VI* ■

Making it work for you

Summary

A democratic environment is supportive for children, staff and parents, and contributes towards positive self-esteem. Caregivers need to feel okay about themselves in order to respond effectively and appropriately to others.

Early childhood workers need to acknowledge the valuable role they have in supporting families, although society in general has a responsibility to provide today's parents with programs which offer knowledge, support and encouragement. An early childhood centre, where parents and caregivers have a unique relationship, is the ideal environment for caregivers to use their skills and understanding to provide effective and responsive programs.

■ *G U I D E L I N E S   F O R   A* ■
S T R U C T U R E D
L E A R N I N G   P R O G R A M

If this book is used as a structured learning module for in-service programs or teaching, principles of Individual Psychology will be demonstrated in the learning situation where a democratic and encouraging atmosphere is provided between participants. Mutual respect for one another is shown through listening, sharing ideas and sharing the time, so acknowledging and allowing each group member equal rights. Through this approach it is expected that the person leading these sessions will model the principles being introduced.

The sessions are designed to have some theory and some written input, with an emphasis on communication and discussion. Participants are likely to feel more comfortable and develop new skills and techniques more effectively by using them initially in a familiar setting with peers. Consequently it is important to allow time for group practice and discussion. Some group members may be unwilling to participate in this until their trust in the group has developed.

1 Structure of content
The content has been organised to meet the needs of people caring for young children and of students in Early Childhood Train-

ing Courses, and to respond to varying placement allocations of these courses. Content may be re-organised to meet the requirements of individuals or other groups.

Each session will focus on either one chapter, or one section of the book, thus retaining continuity and an effective knowledge base.

At the beginning and end of each section, it is important to review and reinforce the content included to allow for the most effective learning to take place.

2 Size of group

The practical component of this book has been designed for groups of about twelve to fifteen participants. Large group numbers may be threatening so consequently a smaller, encouraging and supportive group environment is recommended as being more beneficial.

3 Qualifications of group leader

As this unit is designed to provide participants with the skills and understanding necessary for guiding the behaviour of children, it is appropriate that it is taught by a person qualified in early childhood development and psychology. Moreover, this person will be providing a model for participants through their leadership and interpersonal skills, and so should be able to demonstrate the ideas which are being introduced and developed.

4 Attendance

Participants, who are unable to attend sessions consistently, will find the acquisition of relevant knowledge and the development of appropriate skills difficult without the theoretical understanding, practice sessions, feedback and reinforcement.

Consequently it is desirable that attendance of participants is maximised.

5 Time allotments

The sessions are designed around a two-hour schedule, with or without a break according to individual needs. However, the nature of each group differs and leaders are encouraged to respond to participants' requests and/or feedback. It is important to ensure that there is time to complete the Review and Further learning activities before commencing the next session.

6 Recommended reading

A list of suggested reading is included in most chapters and a full bibliography is listed at the end of the book. As *Understanding Children* emphasises a particular approach, general background reading related to Individual Psychology is invaluable. The book by Maurice Balson, *Becoming Better Parents* provides a simple and practical outline for students, teachers and others working with children.

■ *B I B L I O G A P H Y* ■

Adler, A. 1927, *The Practice and Theory of Individual Psychology*. Harcourt, Brace and Co., N.Y.

Adler, A. 1957, *Understanding Human Behaviour*, Fawcett, N.Y.

Balson, Maurice 1994, *Becoming Better Parents* 4th Edition ACER, Melbourne.

Berger, Eugenia Hepworth 1981, *Parents As Partners in Education*, Mosby Company, U.S.A.

Berk, Laura E. 1989, *Child Development*, Allyn and Bacon, Boston.

Biddulph, Steve 1988, *The Secret of Happy Children*, Bay Books, Sydney.

Bredekamp, Sue 1987, *Developmentally Appropriate Practice in Early Childhood Programs*, NAEYC, Washington.

Curry, Nancy & Johnson, Carl 1992, *Beyond Self-esteem: Developing a Genuine Sense of Human Value*, NAEYC, Washington.

Dinkmeyer, Don & Losoncy, Lewis 1980, *The Encouragement Book: Becoming A Positive Person*, Prentice Hall, N.J.

Dinkmeyer, Don & McKay, Gary 1973, *Raising A Responsible Child*, Simon and Schuster, New York.

Dinkmeyer, Don & McKay, Gary 1976, *Systematic Training for Effective Parenting: Parent's Handbook*, AGS, Circle Pines, Minnesota.

Dinkmeyer, Don, McKay, Gary & Dinkmeyer, James 1989, *Parenting Young Children*, AGS, Circle Pines, Minnesota.

Dreikurs, Rudolf 1985, *Happy Children: A Challenge to Parents*, 10th Edition, Fontana, Great Britain.

Ellis, Albert & Harper, Robert 1975, *A New Guide to Rational Living*, Prentice Hall, N.J.

Erikson, Erik H. 1963, *Childhood and Society*, Penguin Books, London.

Galambos-Stone, Jeannette 1987, *A Guide to Discipline* (Revised Edition), NAEYC, Washington.

Hildebrand, Verna 1975, *Guiding Young Children* Macmillan, New York.

Leavitt, Robin & Eheart, Brenda 1987, *Toddler Day Care: A Guide to Responsive Caregiving*, Lexington Books, Toronto.

Montgomery, Bob & Evans, Lyn 1984, *You and Stress: A Guide to Successful Living*, Nelson, Melbourne.

Piaget, Jean [1928] 1976, *Judgement and Reasoning in the Child*, Littlefield, Adams, N.J.

Satir, Virginia 1987, *People Making*, Souvenir Press, London.

Schnebly, Lee 1987, *Out of Apples: Lighthearted Psychology*, Manzanas Press, Arizona.

Willis, Anne & Ricciuti, Henry 1978, *A Good Beginning for Babies: Guidelines for Group Care*, NAEYC, Washington.

■ *I N D E X* ■